Business Result

Intermediate | Teacher's Book

John Hughes

OXFORD

UNIVERSITY PRESS

Great Clarendon Street, Oxford OX2 6DP

Oxford University Press is a department of the University of Oxford.
It furthers the University's objective of excellence in research, scholarship,
and education by publishing worldwide in

Oxford New York

Auckland Cape Town Dar es Salaam Hong Kong Karachi
Kuala Lumpur Madrid Melbourne Mexico City Nairobi
New Delhi Shanghai Taipei Toronto

With offices in

Argentina Austria Brazil Chile Czech Republic France Greece
Guatemala Hungary Italy Japan Poland Portugal Singapore
South Korea Switzerland Thailand Turkey Ukraine Vietnam

OXFORD and OXFORD ENGLISH are registered trade marks of
Oxford University Press in the UK and in certain other countries

ISBN: 978 0 19 476807 8

Printed in China

ACKNOWLEDGEMENTS

Accompanying Teacher's DVD produced by: MTJ Media, Oxford, UK

*The Publisher would also like to thank the following for their kind assistance with the
accompanying Teacher's DVD*: Andreas Sterz, Branislav Mala, Vanda Loncnarova,
Hazem Alzubairi, Manon Balthazard, Tariq Alyamani, Gianluca Fioretti, Tania
Maria Mendonça Campos, Bill Cheesman, Catriona Davidson (The Eckersley
School of English, Oxford, UK), Tim Bird (British Study Centres, Oxford, UK),
David Newton (OISE, Oxford, UK), Julia Ward (OISE, Oxford, UK), Judith Bolt
(King's School, Oxford, UK), Meriel Steele (Oxford English Centre, Oxford, UK)

Contents

Introduction

The course

Who is *Business Result* for?

Business Result is a comprehensive multi-level course in business English suitable for a wide range of learners. The main emphasis is on *enabling* your students; helping them to communicate more effectively in their working lives.

In-work students

Unlike many business English courses, *Business Result* addresses the language and communication needs of employees at all levels of an organization who need to use English at work. It recognizes that the business world is truly international, and that many people working in a modern, global environment spend much of their time doing everyday tasks in English – communicating with colleagues and work contacts by phone, via email, and in a range of face-to-face situations such as formal and informal meetings / discussions, and various planned and unplanned social encounters. It contains topics relevant to executive-level learners, but doesn't assume that the majority of students will be international managers who 'do business' in English – the activities allow the students to participate in a way that is relevant to them, whatever their level in their company or organization.

Pre-work students

Business Result can also be used with pre-work students at college level. The course covers a variety of engaging topics over the sixteen units, so students without much work experience will receive a wide-ranging overview of the business world, as well as acquiring the key communication skills they will need in their future working lives. Each unit in this *Teacher's Book* contains suggestions for adapting the material to the needs of pre-work students.

One-to-one teaching

Many of the activities in the book are designed for use with groups of students, but they can also be easily adapted to suit a one-to-one teaching situation. Notes in the individual *Teacher's Book* units offer suggestions and help with this.

What approach does *Business Result* take?

Business Result helps students communicate in English in real-life work situations. The priority at all times is on enabling them to do so more effectively and with confidence. The target language in each unit has been carefully selected to ensure that students will be equipped with genuinely useful, transferable language that they can take out of the classroom and use immediately in the workplace.

The course recognizes that, with so many businesses now being staffed by people of different nationalities, there is an increasing trend towards using English as the language of internal communication in many organizations. As well as learning appropriate language for communicating externally – with clients or suppliers, for example – students are also given the opportunity to practise in situations that take place within an organization, such as informal meetings, job appraisals, or social chat.

The main emphasis of the course is on the students speaking and trying out the target language in meaningful and authentic ways; it is expected that a large proportion of the lesson time will be spent on activating students' interest and encouraging them to talk.

The material intentionally takes a communicative, heads-up approach, maximizing the amount of classroom time available to focus on and practise the target language. However, you will also find that there is plenty of support in terms of reference notes, written practice, and review material.

The syllabus is essentially communication-driven. The focus on *Business communication skills* as the core of each unit ensures that students are provided with a range of phrases they can use immediately, both in the classroom and in their day-to-day work. The topics in each of the sixteen units have been chosen because of their relevance to modern business and the world of work. Vocabulary is presented in realistic contexts with reference to authentic companies or organizations. Grammar is also a key element of each unit, ensuring that students also pay attention to accuracy and become more proficient at expressing themselves clearly and precisely.

Student's Book

The Student's Book pack

The *Student's Book* pack offers a blend of classroom teaching and self-study, with an emphasis on flexibility and time-efficiency. Each of the sixteen *Student's Book* units provides around four hours of classroom material with the potential for two to three hours of additional study using other components in the package.

There are no long reading texts in the units, and with an emphasis on listening and speaking, written exercises are kept to a minimum. Instead, students are directed to the *Practice file* at the back of the book; here they will find exercises which can be used as supplementary material in class or for homework, as well as more extensive grammar notes.

Encourage your students to look at and use the *Interactive Workbook* on CD-ROM – there are cross-references at appropriate points in each unit. Here they will find a range of self-study material to help them review, consolidate, and extend their learning.

Writing is a feature of the course, but is not part of the main *Student's Book* units. The *Interactive Workbook* has an email writing section with exercises and model emails related to the content of every unit. There is also a writing file on the *Business Result* website.

Key features of a unit

Each unit has three main sections – *Working with words, Business communication skills* and *Language at work* – dealing with core vocabulary associated with the unit theme, key functional expressions, and related grammar. Each main section ends with a short fluency task to enable students to personalize the target language. Each unit ends with a *Case study* or related *Activity*.

Unit menu

This lists the key learning objectives of the unit.

Starting point

Each unit opens with some lead-in questions to raise awareness of and interest in the unit theme. Use these questions to help you to establish what students already know about the topic and how it relates to their own working lives. They can usually be discussed as a class or in small groups.

Working with words

This first main section introduces key vocabulary in a variety of ways, including authentic reading texts, listenings, and visuals. Students are also encouraged to look at how different forms of words (verbs, adjectives, and nouns) can be built from the same root, or find common collocates that will help them to expand their personal lexicon more rapidly. This section also offers opportunities to work on your students' reading and listening skills. There is a glossary of all target lexis, plus other reference vocabulary, on the *Interactive Workbook* in both PDF and interactive formats.

Business communication skills

This section focuses on one of four broad communication themes – meetings, presenting, exchanging information, and socializing. These are treated differently throughout the book so that, for example, students are able to practise exchanging information on the phone as well as face-to-face, or compare the different language needed for giving formal and informal presentations. Typically, the section begins with students listening to an example situation (a meeting, a presentation, a social encounter, a series of phone calls). They focus on *Key expressions* used by the speakers which are listed on the page. They are then given the opportunity to practise these in various controlled and more open work-related tasks.

Practically speaking

This section looks at various useful aspects of everyday communication from a 'how to' perspective. It covers some of the more informal, but very practical aspects of social interaction in the workplace – for example, being an active listener, ending a conversation, or getting someone's attention.

Language at work

This section focuses on the key grammar underpinning the communication skills section that precedes it. The grammar is reviewed from a communicative point of view; this will meet your students' expectations with regard to learning form and meaning, but also reminds them how the grammar they need to learn commonly occurs in business and work situations. Grammar is taught at this later stage of the unit in order to link it meaningfully to the previously taught vocabulary and phrases.

Case studies

Most units end with a *Case study**. This gives students an opportunity to recycle the language from the unit, demonstrate progress, and use their knowledge and ideas to resolve an authentic problem or issue. The *Case studies* have been compiled using authentic content and the contexts connect with the unit theme. The content is accessible, and preparation time is minimized by including only as much information as can be assimilated relatively quickly in class. Even so, you may wish to optimize classroom time even further by asking students to read the background material before the lesson.

The *Case studies* follow a three-part structure.

Background – a short text (or texts) about a real company, product, or related situation.

Discussion – discussion questions on key issues arising from the background information and associated issues, providing a natural bridge to the task.

Task – a discussion, meeting simulation, or series of tasks, aimed at resolving a core issue related to the case and providing extended practice of the target language of the unit.

*Note that in two units, the *Case study* format is replaced with an *Activity*; a board game (*Unit 3*) and a decision game (*Unit 11*).

Tips

Commonly confused language or language points which may cause difficulty are anticipated by short, practical tips.

Additional material

At the back of the *Student's Book*, you will find the following sections.

Practice file

This provides unit-by-unit support for your classroom work. Each file provides additional practice of target language from the three main unit sections: *Working with words, Business communication skills,* and *Language at work*. This can be used in two ways:

For extra practice in class – refer students to this section for more controlled practice of new vocabulary, key expressions, or grammar before moving to the next stage. The optimum point at which to do this is indicated by cross-references in the *Student's Book* unit and the teaching notes in this book.

For self-study – students can complete and self-check the exercises for review and revision outside class.

Answers for the *Practice file* appear on pages 122–125 of this book, and on the *Interactive Workbook*.

Information files

Additional information for pair work, group activities, and case studies.

Irregular verb list

Audio script

Interactive Workbook

This is a self-study component on CD-ROM. It contains:
- interactive Exercises and Tests for each unit, with answers
- interactive Email exercises, plus a Sample email for each unit
- interactive Phrasebank – students can create their own personalized 'Phrasebook'
- interactive Glossary for students to test their vocabulary
- reference Glossary in PDF format, both Unit by unit and A–Z
- *Student's Book* grammar explanations in PDF format
- *Student's Book* Audio in MP3 format.

For additional practice material, refer your students to the website at **www.oup.com/elt/result**.

Teacher's book

Needs analysis form (pages 126–127)

Use this form to analyse the needs of your learners at the start of the course in order to tailor your approach more closely to their needs.

What's in each unit?

Unit content

This provides an overview of the main aims and objectives of the unit.

Context

This section not only provides information on the teaching points covered in the unit, but also offers some background information on the main business theme of the unit. This will include reference to its importance in the current business world as well as a brief discussion of related issues, such as cross-cultural awareness or technology. If you are less familiar with the world of business, you will find this section especially helpful to read before starting a unit.

Teaching notes and answers

Notes on managing the *Student's Book* exercises and various activities are given throughout, with suggested variations that you might like to try. You will find comprehensive answers to all *Student's Book* exercises, as well as notes on possible responses to discussion questions.

Extension

With some students it may be appropriate to extend an exercise in some way or relate the language point more specifically to a particular group of students. Suggestions on how to do this are given where appropriate.

Extra activity

If you have time or would like to develop further areas of language competence, extra activities are suggested where they naturally follow the order of activities in the *Student's Book*. For example, the *Teacher's Book* may suggest additional comprehension tasks to provide more listening practice and exploit a particular listening activity more fully. Alternatively, if your students need to write emails, extra follow-up ideas are provided.

Alternative

With some students it may be preferable to approach an activity in a different way, depending on their level or their interests. These options are provided where appropriate.

Pronunciation

Tips on teaching pronunciation and helping students improve their intelligibility are provided where there is a logical need for them. These tips often appear where new vocabulary is taught or for making key expressions sound more natural and fluent.

Dictionary skills

It's helpful to encourage students to use a good dictionary in class and the relevant notes suggest moments in the lesson when it may be helpful to develop your students' skills in using dictionaries.

They also offer ideas on how new language can be recorded by students appropriately in their notebooks.

Pre-work learners

Although most users of *Business Result* will be students who are already in work, you may also be teaching classes of students who have little or no experience of the business world. Where necessary, you may want to adapt certain questions or tasks in the book to their needs, and extra notes are given for these types of learners.

One-to-one

In general, you will find that *Business Result* can be used with any size of class. However, with one-to-one students you will find that activities which have been designed with groups of students in mind will need some adaptation. In this case, you may wish to follow the suggested alternatives given in this book.

Feedback focus

Throughout the course, students are involved in speaking activities using the new language. You will want to monitor, correct, and suggest areas for improvement as well as acknowledging successes. During and after many of the freer practice activities it will be helpful to follow the guidelines in the teaching notes on what to monitor for and ways of giving feedback.

Watch out

This is a note to highlight any potentially problematic language points, with suggestions on how to pre-teach certain vocabulary or clear up misunderstandings.

Photocopiable tests (pages 86–117)

There are two types of test to accompany each unit. These can be administered at the end of each unit in order to assess your students' learning and allow you, the student, or the head of training to keep track of their overall progress.

Progress test

Each of these sixteen tests check key vocabulary, key expressions, and grammar for the unit. They provide a final score out of 30. Students will need between fifteen and twenty minutes to complete the test, although you can choose to set a time limit that would be appropriate for your students.

Speaking test

To help you assess communicative performance, students are given a speaking task that closely resembles one of the speaking activities in the unit. Students get a score out of a possible ten marks.

How to manage the speaking test

In most cases, the speaking test is set up as pair work. The pairs carry out two role-plays: Student A is assessed in the first, Student B in the second. The marking criteria require students to perform five functions in the conversation and it is advised that you make students familiar with these criteria beforehand. You can grade each of the five functions using a straightforward scoring system of 0, 1, or 2, giving a final score out of ten. This kind of test can be carried out during the class, perhaps while other students are taking the written progress test, or you can set aside a specific time for testing.

Note that if testing is not a priority, the role-plays can also be used as extra classroom practice without necessarily making use of the marking criteria.

Teacher's Book DVD

The *Teacher's Book* at each level of *Business Result* is accompanied by a *DVD* which demonstrates how sections from the *Student's Book* can be used with a typical group of students. It addresses key issues relevant to the level and looks at various classroom approaches. The *DVD* also includes commentary from teachers and one of the *Student's Book* authors, and addresses many of the questions that teachers have to ask themselves when starting a new business English course. The *Intermediate DVD* uses sections from *Student's Book Unit 5*.

There are a number of different ways to use the *DVD*.

Orientation through the course

Watching the *DVD* is a fast way to familiarize yourself with the course – how the course is organized, its approach to business English, and ways of using the material in the classroom.

Supporting new teachers

If this is your first time teaching business English, you will find watching the *DVD* especially helpful. It provides guidance, advice, and tips on the difference between general English and business English, and suggests approaches to working with business English students.

Teacher development

You may be a more experienced teacher, in which case the *DVD* will address many issues you are already familiar with, but perhaps never have the opportunity to discuss with fellow professionals.

Teacher training

Directors of Studies or teacher trainers will be particularly interested in using the *DVD* as part of a complete teacher-training package. Each *DVD* forms the basis of a training session lasting approximately 45 minutes. You can use the *DVD* in different segments with ready-to-use worksheets on pages 128–133 of this *Teacher's Book* (*Answer key* on pages 134–135) and training notes that are available from the *Business Result* website (see below). Simply photocopy the worksheets and download the training notes to use in conjunction with the *DVD* in your staff training and development sessions. Note that *DVDs* at other levels of *Business Result* address different business English themes; together, the *DVDs* from the different levels form an entire training package in teaching business English. See the website for more information.

Teacher's website

The website can be found at **www.oup.com/elt/teacher/result**. It contains a range of additional materials, including:

- downloadable diagnostic test
- progress test record
- course management & assessment tools
- *DVD* training notes
- wordlists
- additional activities
- writing file.

Using the course

How to use *Business Result*

From start to finish

You can, of course, use *Business Result* conventionally, starting at *Unit 1* and working your way through each unit in turn. If you do so you will find it works well. Each section of the unit is related thematically to the others; there is a degree of recycling and a steady progression towards overall competence, culminating in the *Case study*. Timing will inevitably vary, but allow approximately four classroom hours for each unit. You will need more time if you intend to do the *Practice file* activities in class.

The 'fast-track' option

If you have less time, and wish to focus more on developing your students' communication skills, create a 'fast-track' course using the central section of each unit: *Business communication skills*, and the *Case study*. This will still provide a coherent balance of input and output, and students will spend more of their time actively engaged in using the language. You should find with this option that each unit provides at least two hours of classroom material.

Include *Practically speaking* if you wish – allow approximately 20 to 30 minutes extra. If your students need grammatical support or revision, use as much of the *Language at work* section as you feel is appropriate, or refer students to the reference notes in the *Practice file*.

Mix and match

If your students have more specific needs and you would like to 'cherry pick' what you feel are the most interesting and relevant sections of the book, this approach should work well. You will find that all the sections are essentially free-standing, despite being thematically linked, and can be used independently of the rest of the unit. Mix and match sections across the book to create a course that is tailored to your students' needs.

The Expert View from Cranfield School of Management

Cranfield University School of Management is one of the world's leading business schools, and one of only a small number of schools worldwide designated as 'triple-accredited'. It offers a widely respected international MBA programme, as well as a range of MSc and Executive Development courses.

The partnership between OUP and Cranfield provides authentication for key aspects of the course material, particularly the *Case studies*. Each *Case study* is accompanied by a brief commentary on the topic or issue covered. These short texts are written by members of the School of Management academic staff, leading practitioners in their field, and in some cases by former course participants who work in international business. They offer insights and advice on the *Case study* theme. There is also an introductory section in the *Student's Book* which includes information about Cranfield and some biodata on the contributors.

Further information about Cranfield programmes can be found at: **www.cranfield.ac.uk/som**

Unit content

By the end of this unit, students will be able to

- describe what they like and dislike about their jobs and give reasons why
- talk about responsibilities at work
- introduce themselves and others in a social situation and for networking
- respond to others and show interest in their comments
- use the present simple and frequency adverbs for talking about jobs and activities.

Context

The topic of *Working life* allows for discussion of fairly general work-related issues, and is therefore a good starting point for a course. It's worth remembering how important conversations around this topic will be in your students' working life. Getting to know people and finding out about their lives is a crucial part of the business process. Knowing about the people you do business with helps secure future business. It also helps to build a sense of trust between clients and customers.

The topic also incorporates meeting people for the first time and your students will find it helpful to know what to say in these situations. There are related cultural issues to consider. In some cultures first meetings are quite formal, whereas in other cultures (e.g. the USA) business people will switch to first names straight away. Students will also need to consider which topics are appropriate for discussion. In some cultures people will only discuss work-related issues. However, in other cultures people will discuss more general topics for some time before finding out about each other's roles or responsibilities.

In this unit, students will practise the language needed when meeting new people. They will also have the opportunity to compare their views about the importance of socializing. For students who don't feel that talking about their everyday life is important, you may need to point out that in some countries it is helpful to do so at the beginning and end of meetings or phone calls.

Starting point

Allow time for students to consider their responses to both questions. For the first question students could number the items in the list from one (most important) to eight (least important). They can then compare their answers to both questions with a partner, before feeding back to the rest of the class.

Pre-work learners

Ask students to think about their responses to the first question as if they were at a job interview.

Extension

Students work in pairs. Ask them to think of two more items that are important when choosing a job. For example:

- a company pension scheme
- your own office
- a helpful boss.

Pairs then share their ideas with the rest of the class.

Working with words

1 As a lead-in, ask the class to suggest positive and negative points they think the astronaut in the picture will mention. Write their ideas in two columns on the board. When students are reading they can compare the ideas on the board with what is in the text. Note that views on what is positive or negative may vary. For example, some students may not regard daily exercise as a positive point!

> **Possible answers**
> **positive**: glamorous, varied tasks, regular exercise, never dull, the views
> **negative**: uncomfortable conditions, demanding schedule, routine tasks (maintenance / safety checks), lonely, stressful

Extension

Ask students if any of the positive or negative items listed are also true for their own job. Students can work alone and make a similar list for their job before comparing their list with a partner.

2 01, 02▷ Before playing the listening, check that students understand the word *ambition*. Ask students to think back to their answer to the second question in the *Starting point*. Then ask different students to say what their ambition was when they were young. Find out if anyone has achieved their career ambition.

Watch out! You might need to pre-teach the following:
bureaucracy = the system of official rules and ways of doing things that an organization and government has, especially when these seem to be too complicated
corruption = dishonest or illegal behaviour, especially of people in authority.

Answers
1 Ingrid is an NGO worker.
(NGO stands for Non-Governmental Organization and is an organization that is not run by any government, but which may receive funding for certain projects from a government's development fund.)
Mansour is an air traffic controller.
2 Ingrid likes her work because she sees results and has a sense of achievement. She dislikes it because the bureaucracy and corruption can be depressing.
Mansour likes his work because it's challenging and rewarding. He dislikes it because it can be exhausting.

3 Discuss as a class. There is no right or wrong answer.

Possible answers
Ingrid is helping people in need, so this is similar to being a doctor in some ways.
Mansour's job isn't really like being a pilot, although he works with them.

4 All of these adjectives have appeared in this section already, so students can begin matching straight away.

Answers
1 worthwhile
2 dull
3 demanding
4 challenging
5 fun
6 glamorous
7 routine
8 depressing
9 varied
10 stressful
11 rewarding

Pronunciation
Drill any multi-syllable words in **4** to make sure students know how to say them before the next exercise.

≫ If students need more practice, go to **Practice file 1** on page 102 of the **Student's Book**.

5 After students have described the jobs in pairs, work through the answers for each picture. Ask different pairs to give one of their descriptions to the rest of the class.

6 Students could look at the list in **4** and tick any adjectives which describe their job to help them with this task. Encourage them to think of any more adjectives they know which they can also use. They then work in pairs or groups. Make sure they give reasons for their choice of adjective.

Pre-work learners
Ask students to think about their dream job and describe how they think it will be, using the adjectives.

Alternative
If you think that your students might find this task difficult, write the following structure on the board to help them.
  Being a _____ *(job title) is* _____
  (adjective) because _____ *(reason).*
You could give an example by describing your own job.

Watch out! Note that it can sometimes be difficult to translate a student's job title, so check that everyone knows what it is in English. If the title simply doesn't translate, allow them to begin their description like this: *My job is …*

ⓘ Refer students to the **Interactive Workbook Glossary** for further study.

Business communication skills

1 Discuss these questions as a class. Some other internationally known NGOs include UNICEF and Médecins Sans Frontières. Typically their role is to provide aid and expertise to projects in developing countries.

Watch out! You might need to pre-teach the following:
sponsors = a person or company that helps pay the costs of something, such as a special event or scientific project, usually in order to advertise their products
fundraisers = people who find ways to get money for charities or NGOs.

2 03▷ Before playing the listening, set the scene by asking students to suggest ways they think NGOs might raise money (e.g. collecting money from the public in the streets, membership fees to their organization, approaching big businesses for sponsorship, or holding a fund-raising rock concert). Then check that students know that they have to identify which is a more formal conversation.

Answer

The second listening is more formal for the following reasons: the speakers use titles (*Mr*, *Dr*); they use more formal phrases, such as *I'm delighted to meet you*.

Note that both conversations involve people meeting for the first time and are both acceptable.

Extension

Note that there are cultural issues to be explored in relation to levels of formality. As mentioned in the *Context* section, the use of first names is more typical in a country like the USA, whereas surnames might be preferred in places such as Japan or Germany. Write the following questions on the board for discussion.

- *When meeting someone for the first time, would you normally be more formal or less formal?*
- *Have you experienced different levels of formality at first meetings with people from different cultures?*

3 03▷ Before playing the listening again, point out that not all of the speakers give exact job titles.

Answers
Luc Akele: area manager, in charge of sub-Saharan Africa operations, oversees projects and makes sure money is well spent, reports to main sponsors.
Jo Johansson: deals with fund applications.
Walter Mayer: responsible for medical donations programme, handles inter-government work.

4 Students categorize the phrases. They can then work in pairs to discuss which are more formal or less formal.

Answers
1 e, h
2 a, b, g
3 c, d, f
Phrases c, d, and g are slightly more formal. Phrase f is appropriate in both formal and informal situations.

Extension

Students can work in pairs and practise introducing themselves to each other in two ways – formally and less formally. The class could also stand and move around the room to practise introducing someone else.

5 04▷ Before listening, ask students to predict the missing words in sentences 1–6. They might remember some of the words from the conversations in listening **03▷**.

Answers
1 deal with   4 responsible for
2 in charge of   5 handle
3 oversee   6 involves

» If students need more practice, go to **Practice file 1** on page 102 of the **Student's Book**. Students might need to refer to the *Key expressions*.

Tip Refer students to the *Tip* about *actually*.

Extension

To practise the use of *actually*, ask students to write three things they know are untrue about their partner. Students then take turns to ask a question or make a statement about their partner. Their partner has to correct or contradict them. You can model the target language by saying or writing the following examples on the board.

  A *So I hear you're French.*
  B *Actually, I'm from Belgium.*
  A *So what's your position in the marketing department?*
  B *Actually, I'm in the sales department.*

6 Allow a few minutes for students to choose a job and find suitable words in **B** to describe their responsibilities. Students then work in pairs and take turns to describe the jobs. The other student should guess the job.

Alternative

If you think your students will find this difficult, ask them to write out ten full sentences about the jobs in **A** before completing the task.

7 Allow a minute for students to choose a job from **6** before role-playing the situation. Remind them to make use of the language in the *Key expressions*.

For the second situation, where they use their own job, check that each student has the vocabulary to describe their own job before beginning the role-play.

Pre-work learners

For the second situation, students can choose a job of their own choice, or another job from **6**.

Feedback focus

Focus on the correct use of the words and phrases for describing jobs. Note any errors down and write them on the board afterwards. You can also address issues of formality. For example, one student might say *How do you do?*, when another says *Hi*. Point out that it is usually best to follow the level of formality used by the first speaker.

(i) Refer students to the **Interactive Workbook Email** and **Phrasebank** sections for further study.

Practically speaking

1 You might need to demonstrate how we use phrases to show interest. For example, ask a student to tell you a really interesting fact about themselves, then respond to the comment with *Really?*

> **Answer**
> Phrase 4 isn't a response to show interest – it is generally used to get more information about the other person.

Tip Refer students to the *Tip* about *right* and *really*.

2 Students complete the conversation.

3 05▷ Students listen and check their answers.

> **Answers**
> 1 A recruitment consultant?   4 Oh, right.
> 2 That sounds …   5 Really?
> 3 So tell me, …

4 Allow a few minutes for students to prepare their information before starting their conversations.

Pre-work learners

Students write information about what they are studying or what they hope to do in the future. For example:
> A *I'd like to work in marketing.*
> B *Marketing? That sounds interesting. Why do you want to do that?*

Language at work

1 Students read and answer the questions.

Watch out! You might need to pre-teach the following:
grant = a sum of money that is given by the government or by another organization to be used for a particular purpose.

> **Suggested answers**
> *works* – a general fact
> *focus* – a general truth about the organization's activity
> *visit* – an action often repeated (used with an adverb of frequency)

2 Students match the present simple questions with their use.

> **Answers**
> 1 Sentence b. Sentence d can also be answered *yes / no*, although 2 is more likely.
> 2 Sentences a, c, and d.
> 3 Sentence d is indirect. Check students realize that the verb moves to the end because of the phrase *Can I ask …?* Ask students for other similar expressions: *I'd like to know …*, *Could you tell me …?*, *I was wondering … .*
> 4 Sentences c and d don't use an auxiliary verb. This is because they are questions where the answer is the subject of the question.

>> If students need more practice, go to **Practice file 1** on page 103 of the **Student's Book**.

Extra activity

If students need more help with c (subject questions), write the following on the board.
> *James works for Ford.*

Ask the class to identify the subject and the object.
> *James (subject) works for Ford (object).*

Then write the following.
> *Q1: ……………? Answer: James (subject).*
> *Q2: ……………? Answer: Ford (object).*

Elicit the questions (*Q1: Who works for Ford? Q2: Who does James work for?*). Then highlight the fact that the auxiliary is only needed when the answer is the object.

3 To help students prepare their questions, brainstorm question words or phrases that will help. For example: *how many / how much / how far / what / who / can I ask … ?* While students are talking, they can take notes about their partner to help them with the next exercise.

Feedback focus

Monitor for correct subject or object question forms and the position of the verb in indirect questions.

4 Draw students' attention to the way that *Do you know …?* can begin an indirect question in the same way as *Can I ask …?*, and so it affects the position of the verb.

5 Students order the adverbs on the scale.

> **Answers**
>
>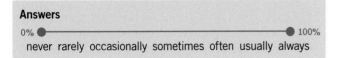
>
> 0% ●————————————● 100%
>
> never rarely occasionally sometimes often usually always

>> If students need more practice, go to **Practice file 1** on page 103 of the **Student's Book**.

6 Students match the adverbs to the phrases.

> **Answers**
> 1 occasionally   4 sometimes
> 2 always   5 rarely
> 3 rarely

7 Students can answer these questions either with an appropriate adverb or the expressions in *italics* in **6**.

Feedback focus

Monitor the position of the adverbs in the sentences.

Extension

Students think of three more similar questions to start off a conversation.

ⓘ Refer students to the **Interactive Workbook Exercises** and **Tests** for revision.

Case study

Background

This *Case study* presents a company that creates situations where business people can make contacts and build relationships. The *Task* involves meetings and introductions, and enables students to practise the language presented in the unit. As this is the first *Case study* of the book, it may be necessary to work through it quite carefully until students become used to the format. As a lead-in, ask the class if they know what *networking* is (making contacts and connections with other potentially useful business people). Students then read the text to find out about *speed networking*. Your students may be interested to know that the idea originated from *speed dating*. This is a similar process, but participants are looking to meet someone for a date rather than for work.

Discussion

1 This question can be discussed as a class.

> **Possible answer**
> Networking is important for companies as it enables them to establish connections with individuals and other companies, who might become clients or partners. It is also important for individuals, as it may help them progress in their careers.

2 Explain that some advantages appear in the text, but they should try to think of more. Students can make lists in pairs before feeding back to the class.

> **Possible answers**
> **advantages**: a fast and efficient form of business networking, a good way to get results, it also sounds fun and means you meet a lot of different people at one event.
>
> **disadvantages**: it costs money to attend, you may not have enough time to decide whether someone is a useful contact, it could be seen as an unnatural way of meeting people.

3 This could be discussed as a class.

> **Possible answers**
> In theory, international speed networking could work via videoconferencing or webcams in order to avoid the problems of travel. Alternatively, it could be combined as part of a conference event over a few days.

Task

1 For experienced business people it might be appropriate to use their own details, although most students will probably prefer to play one of the roles in the *File*. Note that there are seven roles, so that will be the maximum in each group.

2 You could set a time limit of three to four minutes per meeting. Call out (or blow a whistle) to let everyone know their time is up. Give them time to note down the name and score for that person, before meeting someone new.

3 Students can tell the class who they scored highly and why. Feedback should focus on the use of expressions for meeting people and how effectively students interacted.

One-to-one

The student can read the *Background* and go through the *Discussion* section with you. You can both then be one of the people in the *File*, or the student can study the roles and discuss which person might make a useful contact.

>> **Unit 1 Progress test** and **Speaking test**, pages 86–87.

Unit content

By the end of this unit, students will be able to
- talk about different types of projects
- ask for and give updates in a meeting
- delegate tasks in a meeting
- start and end phone calls
- use the present simple and continuous to talk about work and projects.

Context

The topic of *Projects* should have relevance for all learners, since most jobs involve an element of project work, even if it is not labelled as such. Project planning and management is essential, due to the following reasons:
- most projects involve several people with varying expertise, who will need to communicate well and work effectively as a team
- project work usually consists of a series of interrelated tasks, and therefore any task which falls behind schedule will affect the whole project.

A key person in the process is the project manager, who needs to ensure that the project stays within the assigned budget. Part of this will involve keeping delays to a minimum, since falling behind schedule can have enormous financial implications for a business. A project manager will need to
- schedule regular meetings to get updates from team members
- delegate tasks and ensure that people work as a team
- have plans in place for any problems or setbacks.

Issues relating to culture can also arise when working on projects in international teams. The notion of time and its importance varies greatly from culture to culture. Not surprisingly, with projects involving people from different cultures, problems with the perception of time can occur.

In this unit, students will practise the language needed to participate effectively in project meetings. They will also have the opportunity to discuss the problems associated with project work.

Starting point

These questions could be discussed in pairs, groups, or as a class. Possible responses to the first question might include: *good leadership, planning, regular updates on progress, completion within deadlines, the ability to deal with the unexpected.*

Pre-work learners

Write the following questions on the board for discussion.
- *What makes a successful team?*
- *Do you prefer to be part of a team, or to do things on your own?*
- *Think of a time when you planned something with other people, such as a college event or a group presentation. What made it a success / failure?*

Extension

If your students have a lot of experience with project work, you could write the following questions on the board for discussion.
- *Have you ever been involved in a project that went wrong? If so, what happened?*
- *Have you ever worked on a project with people from different cultures? If so, did you experience any difficulties or did you notice any different ways of working?*

Working with words

1 As a lead-in, ask students if they have ever worked for free to help others. Explain that this is *to volunteer*.

Watch out! You might need to pre-teach the following:
to buy into something = to believe in something which other people also believe in.

Answers
1 Volunteerism is a movement within some businesses to encourage staff to offer some of their time and skills for free to help a good cause.

2 Employees in the reading have worked on
- community and social projects
- conservation, teaching, caring, or building
- building an extension to a school
- redecorating a community centre.

3 As well as benefiting the people who receive the help from volunteers, such as the local community, the volunteers themselves also benefit in the following ways:
- gain new skills
- improve teamwork
- gain new ideas and insights
- learn from the experience of others
- learn how to organize a project.

4 Samira has learnt how to organize a schedule and how to deal with a budget.

2 Allow students time to study the items and find the words in the text.

> **Answers**
> | | | | |
> |---|---|---|---|
> | 1 | objectives | 5 | budget |
> | 2 | update | 6 | skills |
> | 3 | schedule | 7 | resources |
> | 4 | deadline | 8 | teamwork |

3 06▷ Before listening, ask students to read the final paragraph of the article again in order to remind themselves of what Samira did.

Students need to listen for the words in **2** and then note more detail about each one. For this reason, you might need to play the listening twice. The first time students write the words, and the second time they make further notes about each one.

> **Answers**
> **1 & 2** deadline – the end of the week
> schedule – they are behind schedule because of the holiday
> resources – at first it was hard to know how to allocate these
> budget – she has stayed within it
> teamwork – it's essential
> update – she receives updates every two days

4 06▷ Students listen again and complete the phrases.

> **Answers**
> | | | | |
> |---|---|---|---|
> | 1 | meet | 6 | allocate |
> | 2 | behind | 7 | within |
> | 3 | up | 8 | delegate |
> | 4 | on | 9 | on with |
> | 5 | ahead of | 10 | get |

Extension

With in-work students, encourage them to describe their own work using the ten phrases and / or to write ten sentences using the phrases.

Tip Refer students to the *Tip*. Check their understanding by asking them the following questions.

> *What time do you start work? Are you always **on time**?*
> *When was the last time you took a flight? Did you arrive at the airport **in time** to do some shopping before checking in?*

5 Allow time for students to read about the situation. Groups could then make a list of points to tell the class. Encourage them to use vocabulary presented in this section.

> **Possible advice for the colleague**
> - meet all the deadlines
> - don't fall behind schedule – if you do, try to catch up and even finish ahead of schedule
> - find out what resources you have and allocate them to your team members
> - always stay within the budget
> - make sure your team members get on with their jobs
> - ask for regular updates from each person in order to maintain control
> - make sure everything is on track

Feedback focus

Focus on any problems with the phrases in **4**. Problems might occur with verb–noun collocations (*meet / deadline*) or the use of prepositions (*be on time / in time*).

Extension

As a follow-up or for homework, students could write an email to the colleague, giving their advice.

» If students need more practice, go to **Practice file 2** on page 104 of the **Student's Book**.

ⓘ Refer students to the **Interactive Glossary** for further study.

Business communication skills

1 07▷ As a lead-in, ask students if they often delegate their work to others. Is this easy or difficult to do? What can go wrong?

Students then need to read the notes on Jaime's note pad before listening. Check that students understand the words *decorating* and *carpet*.

> **Answers**
> decorating – still painting the ceiling, needs another day or so
> lighting – it's finished
> carpets – still waiting, need to call suppliers
> action – meet team to allocate tasks for final stages

2 07▷ Before listening again, students can try and predict the missing words in the phrases.

> **Answers**
> | | | | | | |
> |---|---|---|---|---|---|
> | 1 | are things going | 4 | happening with | 7 | finished that |
> | 2 | so good | 5 | still painting | 8 | to recap |
> | 3 | back on track | 6 | are we with | 9 | to plan |

3 Students categorize the phrases.

> **Answers**
> **a** 1, 4, 6
> **b** 2, 3, 5, 7
> **c** 8, 9

4 Student A will need to use the phrases for asking for an update and summarizing, while Student B will need to give the update. After their first conversation, students can change roles and repeat the dialogue.

> **Tip** To make sure students are confident with the difference in the dates, students work in pairs and tell their partner the dates for the following, in both British and American English:
> • when they started working for their present company
> • their birthday
> • their favourite day in the year (and say why).

5 08▷ Students listen and answer the questions.

> **Answers**
> **1** Bruno
> **2** Josie and Samira
> **3** Josie and Samira

6 08▷ The categorization can be done in pairs.

> **Answers**
> **1** *A*   **6** *D*
> **2** *A*   **7** *O*
> **3** *O*   **8** *A*
> **4** *O*   **9** *D*
> **5** *O*   **10** *S*

>> If students need more practice, go to **Practice file 2** on page 104 of the **Student's Book**. Students might need to refer to the *Key expressions*.

7 Allow a few minutes for students prepare what they will say in this dialogue. Encourage them to underline any key language in sentences 1–10 in **6** that they intend to use. Students can then change roles and repeat the dialogue.

Feedback focus

Focus on the correct use of phrases. Remember to compliment good use of the phrases! You could also ask some pairs to perform their dialogues for the rest of the class.

8 Students could sit back-to-back to simulate a phone call. You don't necessarily need to focus on phrases for telephoning (see the *Practically speaking* section), although

it may be helpful to quickly brainstorm ways of starting and ending a call.

Allow a few minutes for students to read their information before starting. You might need to answer questions about unknown vocabulary. Remind them to make use of the language in the *Key expressions* section.

ⓘ Refer students to the **Interactive Workbook Email** and **Phrasebank** sections for further study.

Practically speaking

1 Students complete the phrases. They can then categorize them in pairs.

> **Answers**
> **1 a** I'm returning your call.
> **c** It's (name) here.
> **e** What can I do for you?
> **f** I'm calling about / for / to …
> **2 b** Thanks for your help.
> **d** Thanks for calling.

Watch out! When calling someone on the phone, students might say *I am* …, or *here is* …, rather than *it is* …, or *this is* … . Point out that this is incorrect and sounds very strange in English. Note also that some nationalities will just say their surname, which sounds very abrupt in English.

2 Students work in pairs and have three phone calls. They can then change roles and repeat the calls so that they practise being both the caller and the receiver.

Alternative

To give students extra practice writing emails, ask them to look at phrases a–f in **1**. Then write the following questions on the board.

> *1 Which phrase can also be used in an email?*
> *2 Which three phrases can be adapted for use in an email?*
> *3 How would you adapt these phrases?*

Suggested answers
1 b
2 a, d, f
3 I'm replying to your email about …, Thanks for emailing / Thanks for your email, I'm emailing about / for / to …

Then ask students to work in pairs and write emails for the situations in **2**. Pairs can then exchange their emails and write responses. If you think your students might find this difficult, you could ask pairs to write each email together before exchanging them with another pair.

Unit content

By the end of this unit, students will be able to
- talk about leisure time and activities
- talk about their work-life balance
- talk about likes and dislikes
- exchange contact details, such as email addresses and telephone numbers
- signal the end of a conversation
- use the past simple and present perfect for talking about past experiences.

Context

The topic of *Leisure time* allows for an extension of some themes introduced in *Unit 1*. In this unit, the themes of meeting people, networking, and making conversations in social situations are revisited and extended. Making contacts is a skill which people need training in, even in their first language, so your students will appreciate having the time to practise using the language needed in these situations.

Another key theme in this unit is work-life balance. In recent years, this has become an important issue in business circles. Electronic communication has allowed more people than ever to work outside the office, and initiatives such as flexitime and homeworking have been developed to allow employees greater freedom. These changes could be seen as beneficial. However, many people believe that we are now more tied to our work than ever before, and that consequently people have less free time for their families or for leisure activities. Many of your students will have experienced the effects of these changes in modern working life.

The first part of this unit deals with language that will help students to make conversations and build relationships. Students also have the opportunity to discuss their own work-life balance. The *Activity* allows students to practise conversational skills in a fun way.

Starting point

Students can discuss these questions in pairs, before feeding back to the rest of the class.

Possible answers
1 Work-life balance is the balance between the time a person spends on work and on leisure.
2 If employees are not expected to work long hours, this might actually improve productivity. Employees could be more motivated and less tired. If employees are less stressed and have fulfilling lives outside work, they might also be less likely to take time off sick or leave the company.
3 Answers will vary. Note that there could also be rules or laws relating to working hours in their countries.

Extension

To extend the discussion, write the following discussion questions on the board.
- *How much leisure time do you have?*
- *What are the working hours at your company?*
- *What kinds of employees would benefit most from working for a company that considers a good work-life balance to be important?*

Students can discuss the questions in pairs before feeding back to the rest of the class. Answers to the third question could include the following.

Parents of young children and older workers might benefit most and people tend to have different priorities at different stages of their lives – they might enjoy working long hours in their twenties, but this might change in their thirties.

Working with words

1 Students read the text and answer the questions. They can then compare their answers in pairs.

Answers
1 In his old job Todd worked fifteen-hour days. In his new job he usually finishes by 5.10 p.m. Students can comment on the hours they work.
2 Todd tells his employees to go home by 5.10 p.m. and not to work at the weekend or take work home.
3 Students comment on their own workplace.

Watch out! If your students all work for the same company, but at different levels, they might not feel comfortable answering the third question. If you think it may be a problem, allow less time for answers and keep the tone good-humoured.

Pre-work learners

Write the following alternative discussion questions on the board.

- *Would you like a boss like Todd?*
- *Do you think companies like Todd's exist in your country or in the area of business you would like to work in?*

2 Allow plenty of time for students to complete the quiz on their own and check what their scores mean in the *File*. Students can discuss whether they agree with the results in pairs or as a class, if you feel no one will be embarrassed by the results.

Watch out! Note that in some cultures, working very long hours is considered the norm and something to be admired. With classes of mixed nationalities this is something to be conscious of. A culture of long hours isn't necessarily something negative. Furthermore some people will choose to work long hours, and if your class includes business-owners and entrepreneurs, expect the balance to be in favour of work.

3 10▷ Each student in the pair focuses on one of the people in the listening. There are no right or wrong answers, but students can identify which of the statements in the quiz the speakers refer to and can guess at the probable responses Nina and Florin would give.

Possible answers (with relevant quotes from listening)
Nina (Student A)
Statement 2 (Score = 1) *I got home at midnight …*
Statement 7 (Score = 0) *I've still got five days holiday left from last year …*

Florin (Student B)
Statement 5 (Score = 2) *Did you go out again last night?*
Statement 6 (Score = 1) *… this Saturday … I'll join him and the sales team from Kyoto for golf.*
Statement 7 (Score = 2) *I used it* (holiday) *all for my walking tour in Morocco.*

Florin appears to have a slightly better work-life balance than Nina because he manages to take his holiday and he has free time to watch TV. Nina has to work late and has difficulty finding time for leisure.

4 If students need help, you could play the listening again so that they can listen for the collocations.

Answers
1	do	3	work
2	take	4	make

Extension

Students could try to think of at least one more noun to add to the lists in 1–4. For example, *do sport / homework / yoga*, *take lunch / a break / a taxi*, *work long hours / online*, *make a mistake / friends*. You could also ask them to look up the verbs in a dictionary and find more examples.

5 Students make sentences in pairs, before feeding back to the rest of the class.

Watch out! You might need to pre-teach the following:
exciting = causing great interest, happiness, or enthusiasm
exhilarating = causing somebody to feel very happy and excited.

6 Note that the responses students give to the activities in the picture will be subjective. For example, a student might describe cycling as either *boring* or *relaxing*.

Pronunciation

The word stress in some of these adjectives is unpredictable and the spelling of *interesting* and *frightening* will suggest to students that they have more syllables than they really do. Ask students to identify how many syllables are in each word (except *hard work*) and to mark the word stress. You might need to read the words aloud. Write the answers on the board.
Answers: *ex**ci**ting* (3) *bo**ring* (2) *re**la**xing* (3) *ex**hi**larating* (5) *ti**ring* (2) *in**te**resting* (3) *fri**gh**tening* (2) *en**jo**yable* (4).

7 Ask students to think of at least four activities. They can then prepare their sentences before working with a partner.

8 11▷ It can be difficult for students to know when to use adjectives with an *-ing* or *-ed* ending. Before listening again, ask students to read sentences 1–3 and see if they can remember which adjectives the speakers used.

Answers
1 tired
2 excited
3 boring
Having completed this, students should be able to answer the question as follows:
The *-ed* form describes how a person feels.

» If students need more practice, go to **Practice file** 3 on page 106 of the **Student's Book**.

Tip Refer students to the *Tip* about *really* and *so*.

9 As a lead-in, write the following activities on the board.
long walks   the dark   history   my next holiday   TV
long hours

Students can work in pairs to match the adjectives + prepositions from **9** to these activities and make sentences.
e.g. *I'm bored with watching TV, … interested in history, … frightened of the dark, … excited about my next holiday, … exhilarated by long walks, … tired of long hours.*

Students can then think of other examples. Draw attention to the fact that all the adjectives listed here end in *-ed* and so describe how people feel.

10 You could demonstrate this activity by describing your responses to the list. For example:
I'd like to work about 30 hours a week with only one day a week in the office. My ideal type of job would be …

Remind students to use the adjectives from this section when explaining how the ideal work-life balance would make them feel.

Feedback focus

Focus on any misuse of *-ing* / *-ed* endings and verb + noun collocations. If you worked on word stress earlier in **6**, you could also focus on this.

ⓘ Refer students to the **Interactive Workbook Glossary** for further study.

Business communication skills

1 12▷ Before listening, ask students if they have *placements* at their companies. Companies sometimes have them for students who need work experience. Other *placements* could involve an employee spending some time in another division of their company.

> **Answers**
> **Department in week 1:** human resources
> **Department in week 2:** marketing
> **Travel to:** Copenhagen
> **Weekend plans:** go to the country with Kris
> **Need to buy:** a few things for the room

2 12▷ Students complete the questions. They then try to remember Mirella's answers. If they find this difficult, they can listen again.

> **Answers**
>
> | Questions | Mirella's responses |
> | --- | --- |
> | **1** Do you like | *Yes, it's great.* |
> | **2** Is this | *Yes, it's my first time out of Brazil.* |
> | **3** What sort of | *Walking around the city.* |
> | **4** How is | *It's fine.* |
> | **5** How do you find | *… the family has been very nice.* |

Watch out! Draw attention to the phrase *How do you find …?* and explain that this is idiomatic. It is used here to ask for someone's opinion.

3 Students works in pairs. Allow time for them to decide on the country and department. They then take turns to ask and answer using the language in **2**.

4 12▷ This exercise develops students' ability to talk about interests without being restricted to *I like / I don't like*. Students match the phrases and then listen again to check their answers.

> **Answers**
> **1** 's interested in
> **2** 's fond of
> **3** isn't crazy about
> **4** isn't keen on

Tip Refer students to the *Tip* about *like* + *-ing*, or the infinitive. You could extend this language point by writing the following verbs on the board.
enjoy   hate   love   keen on

Ask the class if the verbs can be followed by *to*, *-ing*, or both. Refer them to the *Key expressions* list to find out if they are correct.
Answers: *enjoy + -ing, hate + -ing / to, love + -ing / to, keen on + -ing.*

5 Students work in pairs to practise the new phrases for describing likes / dislikes.

6 13▷ Students listen and complete the notes.

> **Answers**
> Extension no: 351
> Press 9 for an outside line.
> Company no.: 00 46 096 745 6745
> Email: mirella_2@dipris.se
> Mirella checks her spelling by clarifying it with names of everyday objects (S for sugar, E for egg).

7 Students can choose their own email addresses and numbers, or they can think of ones they often use at work. If they are unfamiliar with the words to describe email addresses, refer them to the *Key expressions* list. Note that we tend to say telephone numbers in groups of two or three numbers. The pause between each group allows the listener time to write them down.

» If students need more practice, go to **Practice file 3** on page 106 of the **Student's Book**. Students might need to refer to the *Key expressions*.

8 Students work in pairs and role-play the situation.

Feedback focus

Focus on question forms and the use of expressions to describe likes and dislikes.

ⓘ Refer students to the **Interactive Workbook Email** and **Phrasebank** sections for further study.

Practically speaking

1 Students can sometimes sound abrupt when they try to end a conversation, so they need to know phrases that will enable them to do this appropriately. Students work alone to decide which phrases can end a conversation.

2 14▷ Students listen and check their answers. You could also ask students in what contexts they might use the remaining phrase.

> **Answers**
> Anyway, I'd better get on.
> I need to go now, I'm afraid.
> I should get back to work.
>
> Possible context for the other phrase: I'll get back to him in a minute = referring to calling someone back.

3 14▷ Students listen again and note the responses.

> **Answers**
> Yes, me too.
> OK. Thanks for your help.
> OK. Thanks for calling.

4 Students can work in groups, or you could ask everyone to stand and walk around the room starting different conversations and ending them. You could set a time limit for each conversation (one minute). Call out the end of the minute each time so that students end their conversations and move to the next person.

Language at work

1 Students will probably think of questions in the past simple or present perfect, although this is not essential at this stage.

> **Possible questions**
> How was your holiday? Did you enjoy the conference?
> Have you ever been to Spain? Have you ever been to Japan?

2 15▷ Students listen for the responses in **1** and write the four questions.

> **Answers**
> How was you weekend? Good thanks.
> Did you go to the gallery on Saturday? Yes, I did. It was fascinating.
> Have you ever been there? Yes, a couple of times.
> Have you met Mirella? No, I haven't.

Extension

Ask students to identify the two tenses used in these questions (past simple and present perfect).

3 15▷ To decide if these sentences are true or false, students will need to listen carefully for the tenses used in the listening, as this will affect their answers.

> **Answers (with relevant extract from listening)**
> 1 F (*I've only just arrived.*)
> 2 T (*Yes, I did.*)
> 3 F (*Have you ever been there? Yes, a couple of times.*)
> 4 T (*Have you met Mirella? No, I haven't.*)
> 5 T (*I've just organized a desk for you …*)
> 6 F (*Leif played tennis at the weekend.*)
> 7 T* (*I haven't played for ages.*) *We don't know the exact date.

While discussing the answers and the reasons why 1, 3, and 6 are false, point out the following:
- with the past simple we know when the action happened
- with the present perfect it isn't always clear when the action happened
- we also use the present perfect to talk about recent actions / events.

4 Students match the sentences with the meanings. They can then compare their answers in pairs.

> **Answers**
> 1 c   3 a
> 2 d   4 b

5 Explain that we typically use *since* and *for* with the present perfect.

> **Answers**
> I haven't played tennis for ages. = *for* + a period
> I haven't seen you since January. = *since* + a specific time

Tip Refer students to the *Tip*. For extra practice, ask students to work in pairs and create their own four-line dialogue similar to the example given here.

6 Students work in pairs and choose the correct answer.

> **Answers**
> 1 booked
> 2 Have you ever been
>   Note: it could be *Did you go* if the speaker knows that it had been planned at one stage, but is unsure if the trip happened in the end.
> 3 lived
> 4 haven't seen
> 5 changed
> 6 Did you go
> 7 for
> 8 since

›› If students need more practice, go to **Practice file 3** on page 107 of the **Student's Book**.

7 These questions should generate use of the past simple and present perfect.

Feedback focus

Focus on the correct use of the two tenses. Note down any sentences with mistakes and write them on the board at the end along with any examples of correct sentences. Ask the class to identify the sentences with the errors.

ⓘ Refer students to the **Interactive Workbook Exercises** and **Tests** for revision.

Activity

Unlike most of the units in this book, which end with a *Case study*, this unit uses a board game to practise the target language. Each group will need a dice to roll, or they can use a coin (heads = move one square, tails = move two squares). Each student will also need a counter, such as a coin or small object.

Rather than explain the game, let students read the instructions and organize themselves. Your role can simply be to check they are following the stages correctly. As with any board game, the aim is to reach the END square first, but some squares will move the player forward or backwards and players also have to move to join other players on the board in order to make conversations.

Feedback focus

One way to give feedback is to note any errors on a sheet of paper for each group. Many of your comments will focus on the accuracy of question forms. At the end, give the group its error sheet and let them discuss the mistakes as a group. If you have a lot of groups to monitor, you could introduce the rule that participants in the group must monitor each other's questions. If the group points out a mistake, that player could miss a go or go back one square. More competitive groups with a sense of team spirit and fun will enjoy this variation.

›› Unit 3 Progress test and Speaking test, pages 90–91.

3 18▷ S
listeni

Answ
1 c
2 e
3 a
4 h

4 Stude
answ

Answ
a 1
b 4

» If stu
108 o
the *K*

5 Stude
using

Pos:
2 A
c
3 I
i
4 S
i
5 T
c
6 C
c

6 You
You

MF

Be
sto
sm
allc

Stud

Pos:
File
Be:
les
les
les
eas

Unit content

By the end of this unit, students will be able to
- talk about services and systems
- explain how something works
- introduce information
- make comparisons.

Context

The topic of *Services & systems* has great relevance in the current business climate. Many economies have shifted from being production or manufacturing-based to becoming reliant on service-based industries. Services now account for a higher proportion of the US GDP than they did twenty years ago. Basing a country's economy on the service industry may be a risky policy if basic requirements, such as food, clothing, and fuel are all imported from other countries. However, the trend for major economies to relocate their manufacturing to countries with cheaper labour markets continues.

Technology has also brought about great changes in both services and systems. The Internet has allowed for many new online services, such as online banking. The emphasis is always on making the customer's life easier, but in reality this may not always be the case and you may wish to explore this with your students. In fact many critics say the customer receives worse service than ever before.

With new services come new systems – both for the consumer and for the people who work within companies. When a business tries to improve a system, a manager may have to explain the reasons for a new way of doing something and convince their team that this will be beneficial. Similarly, those working in the service industry will need to be able to persuade sceptics that their life will be better if they buy a new service or if they change the way they have always done something. This unit presents language that will enable students to present new information effectively and persuasively.

Starting point

You might want to describe a service you often use, to help start off the discussion. For example:
> *Dry cleaning service: I like the speed with which they clean and the friendliness of the staff. They also offer a special deal where they clean three suits for the price of two.*

Allow a few minutes for students to make a list of services they use. Students can discuss their answers in pairs before feeding back to the rest of the class.

Extension

To extend the discussion, write the following questions on the board.
- *How much of your country's industry is based on services, rather than manufacturing?*
- *Is this a good or bad thing?*
- *Do you have any real examples of poor customer service?*

Students can discuss in pairs before feeding back to the rest of the class.

Working with words

1 The website reviews describe three different services. One review is about an information search / online news service which would normally be used by businesses who wanted to track what is being said about them in the press or online. The other two reviews refer to the more conventionally known services of online banking and travel booking services.

After students have read the reviews, they can answer the questions.

Answers
1 The first (a) is about The Guardian (a newspaper).
   The second (b) is about Lloyds TSB (a bank).
   The third (c) is about Expedia.com (an online travel agency).
2 Answers will vary.

2 16▷ Each speaker describes a problem or need that they have.

Answers
Speaker 1: website c (travel)
Speaker 2: website b (banking)
Speaker 3: website a (information search / online news)

3 Note that the aim here is not to underline every adjective (such as *new*), but only the adjectives that we typically use to describe and promote services.

Possible answers
user-friendly, up-to-date, accurate, immediate, convenient, secure, time-saving, efficient, cost-effective

Extension

Play the listening again. Then drill the class to give students practice saying the sentences with the correct stress and pausing. Alternatively students could work in pairs, taking turns to say the sentences. Students won't necessarily be perfect, but the exercise will raise their awareness of the importance of these pronunciation features when presenting information.

2 Students match the sentences to the functions to check their understanding.

> **Answers**
> a 3   d 2
> b 5   e 4
> c 1

3 Students pick an object in the classroom or office (or even from their pocket or bag) and instantly present it to their partner.

Alternative

Set the task in **3** for homework. This will give students time to personalize the task by choosing something relevant to their job, e.g. a process or new system. It will also give students more time to practise using the introductory phrases.

Language at work

1 As a lead-in, ask students how their company gets feedback either from staff or from customers. Do they use feedback forms? With pre-work students, ask where they often see feedback forms (e.g. in restaurants or hotels). Your students are probably reasonably familiar with the basic comparative adjective form, so the initial exercises should serve as revision and an opportunity to deal with any gaps in understanding.

> **Answers**
> 1 longer   4 more positive
> 2 easier   5 better
> 3 slow

2 Students need to think about the intensifiers in sentences 1–5 to help them decide how large or small the improvements have been.

> **Answers (with reasons given from comments)**
> 1 no improvement (*takes a little longer to learn how to use*)
> 2 small improvement (*slightly easier to find*)
> 3 big improvement (*definitely not as slow*)
> 4 big improvement (*they are far more positive*)
> 5 big improvement (*it's a great deal better*)

3 Students can work in pairs. If they find this difficult you can refer them to the language reference section in *Practice file 4* at this point.

> **Answers**
> 1 much noisier (not *more*)
> 2 not as dark as (not *darker*)
> 3 bigger (not *biger*)
> 4 much more convenient (not *convenienter*)
> 5 much worse (not *much more worse*)
> 6 as good as (not *as good than*)
> 7 than me (not *that me*)

When checking the answers in **3**, encourage students to give grammatical explanations for their answers.

4 You might need to refer students back to the sentences in **1** to help them categorize the intensifiers.

> **Answers**
> slightly (S), a great deal (B), nearly as … as (S), not anything like as … as (B), a little (S), significantly (B), far more (B), much less (B), marginally (S), not nearly as … as (B), a lot (B)

» If students need more practice, go to **Practice file 4** on page 109 of the **Student's Book**.

5 Student A's questions are given in the feedback form, but Student B is required to create sentences using the adjective in brackets and an intensifier to indicate the level of improvement. If B has problems thinking of a response, suggest that they think of their local supermarket and how good / bad the service is there. Students then change roles and repeat the exercise.

6 It might be helpful to give examples from your present and previous job in order to illustrate the target language.

Alternative

If the context in **6** is not appropriate (for example, students haven't had a previous job or they are pre-work students), the following contexts could replace the situation given:
- compare your current course or college with your last one
- compare your current flat / house with your last one
- compare your English now with the same time last year.

Note that students may have to use other adjectives for these contexts.

Feedback focus

Monitor and give feedback on correct / incorrect use of comparative forms and of intensifiers.

ⓘ Refer students to the **Interactive Workbook Exercises** and **Tests** for revision.

Case study

Background

This *Case study* presents Nike's relocation and how this resulted in the introduction of a new system to encourage employees to leave their cars at home. Many companies are now considering the impact that commuting has on the environment, and this situation provides the context for the *Task*. Students then present information and ideas for a new system, using the language presented in the unit.

Allow a few minutes for students to read the text and be prepared to answer any questions about vocabulary.

Discussion

1 Students can discuss the question in pairs before feeding back to the rest of the class.

> **Possible answers**
> 1 As well as receiving financial incentives for not driving to work, employees also benefit by not having the stress of driving to work. On the bus they can relax and read, or they can get fit and healthy by cycling to work. As the company also pays 72% of bus and rail passes they save money.
> 2 The company benefits by saving money on parking facilities and by being seen as environmentally friendly.
> 3 The local community benefits by having fewer cars on the road, therefore having less congestion and pollution.

2 Students can brainstorm ideas in pairs or as a class.

> **Possible answers**
> Some more ways to reduce the number of cars even further could be to:
> • penalize car drivers (they have to pay to park)
> • provide buses to pick workers up
> • provide information about which employees live near each other, so that drivers can pick each other up
> • implement more ways for staff to work from home, so that on some days they don't need to travel in to work.

3 Students can discuss this in pairs before feeding back to the rest of the class.

Task

1 Allow time for students to read about the commuting situation.

2 Note that the *Files* give figures, but when students report back they should be trying to use some of the language presented in *Language at work*. So rather than saying *36% of staff use public transport compared to 59% last year …*, they can say, *significantly fewer members of staff now use public transport … .*

3 When students think of ways to improve the situation they can use some of the ideas from the Nike situation and the *Discussion* section.

4 Students prepare a presentation of their proposals. When everyone has presented, the class can vote on the best plan. Feedback should focus on how effectively students presented their ideas.

One-to-one

Follow the *Case study* as given, with the student playing Student A and you taking the role of Student B in the *Task*.

➤➤ **Unit 4 Progress test** and **Speaking test**, pages 92–93.

Unit content

By the end of this unit, students will be able to
- talk about customer service
- ask for further information about a product or service
- make, suggest, and change arrangements
- start a conversation on the phone
- use the present simple and continuous for talking about the future
- manage customer feedback.

Context

The topic of *Customers* and customer service will mean different things to different people, depending on their background and culture. The influence of customer care on business success can be enormous. Word of mouth is a powerful tool and people are much more likely to talk about bad customer service than good. Companies will often go to extraordinary lengths to make sure the customer is satisfied. Companies that don't show so much care towards their customers may well suffer, regardless of how good their product is. However, the extent to which a company's customer care affects its sales can vary according to national or company cultures and expectations. In some cultures the service you receive is a major factor in your opinion of the supplier or producer, and may affect your decision to keep working with them. In other cultures, as long as the product or service does what it's meant to do, at the right price, the quality of the customer care received is not considered to be so important.

The first part of this unit deals with the language students will need to be effective when dealing with customers. Students will also have the opportunity to discuss the issues outlined above throughout the unit. The *Case study* offers students the opportunity to think about ways of improving customer care and the *Task* enables students to extend this discussion whilst practising the language presented in the unit.

Starting point

These discussion questions raise the point that everyone is a customer at work in some context. For example, a supplier will have many different external customers, whilst a PA will have an internal customer – his / her boss. Students work in pairs and discuss the questions before feeding back to the rest of the class. If students have problems thinking of answers for **2**, ask them to imagine that they suddenly disappear from work for a week. Who would be affected by their absence? This should provide them with a list of internal customers.

> **Possible answers**
> **external customers**: visitors to a shop, trade customers, online customers.
> **internal customers**: contact in sales office in Hong Kong, boss, receptionist, warehouse manager.

Pre-work learners

Ask students to think of their own school, college, or university. How do they feel as customers there?

Extension

Write the following discussion questions on the board.
- *Do you feel that you are a customer where you work?*
- *Is it important to treat external and internal customers in the same way?*

Students can discuss the questions in pairs before feeding back to the rest of the class.

Working with words

Extra activity

As an extra activity before students start reading, write the following numbers on the board.

1983   2000   2004   2006   20,000   30,000

Read the text about Technogym aloud. Students listen and make notes on what the numbers refer to. They then open their books and check if their notes are correct.

1 Allow a few minutes for students to read the information.

Watch out! You might need to pre-teach the following:
rehabilitation = the process of returning to a normal life after having been very ill or injured
Paralympics = Olympic games for disabled people.

Answers
Technogym produces fitness and biomedical rehabilitation equipment.
The customers mentioned are the fitness centres, private homes, and the Olympics.

2 Students complete the website homepage.

Answers
1	services	4	expectations
2	satisfaction	5	requirements
3	care		

Watch out! Students might ask why the website page uses the plural forms of the words *expectations* and *requirements*. Point out that we assume customers will have more than one of each.

Dictionary skills

If your students need help completing **2**, encourage them to find the words in their dictionaries. To develop their skills with an English–English dictionary, ask everyone to look up the word *serve*. Ask them how the dictionary indicates the verb form and the noun form. They can also look for any other forms of the word.

Pronunciation

Following on from **2**, draw students' attention to the similarities and differences in word stress between the verb and noun forms. Write the following words on the board and say them.

serve, services, satisfy, satisfaction, expect, expectations, require, requirements

Students underline the stressed syllable. They can check their answers by finding the marked word stress in their dictionaries.

3 Allow a few minutes for students to read the sentences and be prepared to clarify the meaning of *treadmill*.

Answers
1	3	4	5
2	2	5	4
3	1		

4 This table allows students to focus on the word families. Students can complete the table alone before comparing their answers with a partner.

Answers
1	service(s)	5	expectation(s)
2	satisfaction	6	requirement(s)
3	supplier	7	production
4	care		

5 Students complete the text. Sometimes more than one answer is possible.

Answers
1	expect	6	expectations / requirements
2	supply	7	services / care
3	services	8	service
4	satisfied	9	cares
5	expectations / requirements	10	products

6 The context of the verbs on the website page should allow students to complete questions 1–6.

Answers
1	require	4	ensure
2	assess	5	provide
3	monitors	6	tailor

» If students need more practice, go to **Practice file 5** on page 110 of the **Student's Book**.

Tip Refer students to the *Tip* about *customer*, *client*, and *consumer*.

7 Allow plenty of time for this. Students can then feed back to the rest of the class.

Pre-work learners

Ask students to think of somewhere where they regularly buy goods and services. They then answer the questions in **6** as they think this retailer would.

8 Allow plenty of time for students to prepare on their own before asking them to present their product. If necessary, set this task as homework. Students can then give their presentations in the next lesson.

Alternative

Students work in groups to present their products, rather than giving more formal individual presentations. Students then compare their products or services.

ⓘ Refer students to the **Interactive Workbook Glossary** for further study.

Business communication skills

1 **20▷** As a lead-in, ask students to brainstorm all the facilities you might find in a hotel. For example: *sauna, mini-bar, gym, restaurant, movie-order channels, masseur, solarium, car park,* etc. Then ask the class which facilities they would expect to find and which would be a nice surprise.

Students listen and complete the notes. They don't need to write the questions in full.

> **Answers**
> 1 Type of hotels 3 Number of hotels
> 2 Age of current facilities 4 Budget

2 **20▷** Before listening again, you could ask students to predict the missing words.

> **Answers**
> 1 find out about 4 deal with
> 2 tell me 5 possible for
> 3 interested in

3 Allow time for Student B to prepare phrases for getting information and Student A to prepare questions about the type and number of hotels, the age of the facilities, and the budget. Refer them back to the phrases for starting and ending calls on page 15 if necessary. Students can sit back-to-back, or if they have mobile phones they can call each other. They then change roles.

Feedback focus

Focus on correct question forms and phrases for getting information. Note that the target phrases include a number of prepositions (*find out about, interested in, deal with, possible for*) and students might make mistakes with these. As you monitor, listen and write down both correct phrases and phrases with errors. Afterwards, write them on the board and ask the students to identify the correct expressions and to correct the mistakes in others.

4 **21▷** Students listen and answer the questions.

> **Answers**
> 1 a meeting
> 2 the start of Sergio's trip
> 3 Elena and Sergio's meeting

5 **21▷** Before listening again, you could ask students to predict the missing words.

> **Answers**
> 1 arrange 3 'd prefer
> 2 How 4 suits

Watch out! Students may ask about the use of *the* in answer 3, since days of the week don't normally need *the*. It is used here because it is a specific Wednesday (the one in the same week as the suggested Tuesday). Students might also have difficulty with the pronunciation of the word *suits* in 4. If necessary, model and drill this a couple of times.

6 Go through the flow chart as a class and elicit the phrases students might use at each stage of the conversation. Students work in pairs. As in the previous role-play, students can work back-to-back. Students can then change roles and repeat the dialogue.

Watch out! Make sure that students write down any dates and times so that they can refer to them when they want to change their arrangements in **9**.

Feedback focus

Focus on the structure of the calls and the correct use of the phrases for making and changing arrangements.

Extension

Ask students to talk about appointments they often have and reasons they have to make arrangements. You could have further role-plays similar to those in **6**, but this time using the students' own real-life contexts as the basis for the call.

Tip Refer students to the *Tip* about *make*.

7 **22▷** Students should notice that Sergio and Elena make general conversation at the beginning of the call. This aspect of telephone calls is expanded in *Practically speaking*.

> **Answers**
> 1 to change the time of their appointment
> 2 work in general and the weather
> 3 Wednesday
> 4 the appointment (to Thursday)

» If students need more practice, go to **Practice file 5** on page 110 of the **Student's Book**. Students might need to refer to the *Key expressions*.

8 Point out to students that the phrasal verbs *bring forward* and *move back* are both separable. This means the object can go between the verb and the participle, as well as after it. Write the following on the board if necessary.
> *bring forward the meeting* ✓
> *bring the meeting forward* ✓
> *move back the visit* ✓
> *move the visit back* ✓

Answers
26th: Meeting at 9.30 a.m.
28th: Tour at 3.00 p.m.

9 Students repeat their role-plays from **6**. Again, go through the flow chart and ask students to suggest possible expressions beforehand. Refer students to the *Key expressions* list to help them.

Feedback focus

Focus on how effective the telephone calls are. Ask students to think about any problems they had and discuss possible causes of those problems.

(i) Refer students to the **Interactive Workbook Email** and **Phrasebank** sections for further study.

Practically speaking

1 23▷ As a lead-in, you could ask students whether they usually make small talk on the telephone. Note that in some cultures people do not use much small talk on the phone, whilst in other cultures it is considered very important for relationship-building with a client or colleague.

Students match the phrases and responses and then listen to check their answers.

Answers

1	e	4	b
2	c	5	d
3	a		

2 Before starting the role-plays, students might find it helpful to think of a realistic context for the phone call. Brainstorm a few ideas for why they might need to call a colleague or client. Students can choose one of these contexts and then begin the role-play, using small talk phrases.

Extension

Ask students how they would answer questions 3 and 4 in **1** at the moment. Then discuss when they have busy periods at work. Then look at different ways to describe the weather, e.g. *rainy, sunny, cloudy, warm*, etc.

Language at work

1 24▷ Before listening, you could ask students to predict the answers.

Answers

1	're coming	3	'm calling
2	comment	4	begins

2 This exercise encourages students to focus on the future use of the present simple and continuous.

Answers
1 and 4

3 Students should now think about the differences between these two sentences.

Answers

a	1	b	4

4 Students complete the sentences.

Answers

1	continuous	2	simple

⟫ If students need more practice, go to **Practice file 5** on page 111 of the **Student's Book**.

5 Students complete the email. They can then compare their answers in pairs.

Answers

1	'm writing	3	arrives
2	are meeting	4	is coming

6 Students work in pairs and think of sentences using the verb + noun combinations. You might need to give them one or two example sentences to start them off.

Tip Refer students to the *Tip* about action and state verbs.

Feedback focus

In this exercise students should be using the grammar they have just learnt as spontaneously as possible. Note down any mistakes you hear and write them on the board afterwards. Ask students to correct the mistakes. If you feel it will help, ask students to change partners and do the exercise again.

(i) Refer students to the **Interactive Workbook Exercises** and **Tests** for revision.

Case study

Background

This *Case study* presents a situation where poor customer service in a hotel resulted in negative online reviews. The topic allows students to consider how this kind of feedback can affect businesses and encourages them to think of how companies should deal with these situations. The *Task* enables them to discuss these issues and practise the language presented in the unit.

As a lead-in, brainstorm what makes a good hotel. Students might have some interesting stories about their own experiences of customer service in hotels. Then allow students a few minutes to read the brochure and the customer feedback.

Discussion

1 Students can discuss these questions in pairs.

> **Possible answers**
> Customers would expect a peaceful location, excellent food, and personalized service. The reviews suggest that customers don't receive expected levels of service and food quality.

2 Students can discuss this in pairs, before feeding back to the rest of the class.

> **Possible answers**
> Most students will probably agree that it is important to act on customer feedback and to see it in a positive way since it can help a business to improve. Many businesses are very customer-driven and rely on feedback to help them to be customer-focused. For hotels, negative online feedback can now really affect business, since many potential guests tend to search for online reviews. However, it is also worth noting that the negative feedback for Limewood Spa may be isolated cases. In this case the hotel might need to look into the issues before reacting too quickly to a couple of negative comments.

3 This question can be discussed in pairs or as a class.

> **Possible answers**
> The feedback suggests that staff at Limewood Spa need training in customer service, as they all criticize employees. The food at the restaurant also receives poor feedback.

Task

1 Students work in pairs. Allow time for students to read their *Files* before they role-play the call.

2 Students now brainstorm ideas at the arranged meeting. They should make a note of their ideas.

3 Pairs present their ideas to the class. Feedback should focus on how effectively the students communicated. They should have practised asking for information and making arrangements. You could also focus on how realistic all their ideas were.

One-to-one

Follow the *Case study* as given, with the student playing Student A and you taking the role of Student B in the *Task* section.

>> **Unit 5 Progress test** and **Speaking test**, pages 94–95.

Unit content

By the end of this unit, students will be able to
- talk about business travel
- explain reasons for a visit
- welcome visitors to their place of work both formally and less formally
- make and respond to offers
- use modals and other verbs for obligation and necessity for talking about work regulations.

Context

The topic of *Guests & visitors* is still important within the business world. Despite increased communication via electronic means (e.g. video conferencing), more people are taking flights than ever before. A huge proportion of a business person's working life can now be taken up with travel. Typical reasons for travel would include attending a conference or an exhibition, visiting a client, or perhaps visiting a division of a company in another country.

Students need language to enable them to function effectively on business trips. They also need to be able to talk about travel with colleagues. Whether travelling or hosting a visit, students need social language so that they can meet and greet. They will also need to be aware of appropriate levels of formality. Part of a visit may also include a tour of a company's technical areas or factories, in which case students will need to understand rules and obligations for their safety and security.

In this unit, students will focus on the language needed in the social situations that arise on business trips. The unit also deals with the language needed for describing rules and regulations. In addition, there are opportunities to discuss the impact of frequent travel on business people and the importance of intercultural awareness when hosting visits or travelling to other countries.

Starting point

When organizing the students for this opening discussion try to make sure that each group includes people who regularly travel for business or who have experience of welcoming visitors to their place of work. If a group doesn't feel they can answer every question, encourage them to move on to the next.

Pre-work learners

Write the following on the board.
- *List the reasons why someone might visit a company.*
- *Think of ways in which you might entertain them in the evening.*
- *What are the pros and cons of travel (for business or leisure)? What can go wrong?*
- *Tell your partner about your travel experiences.*

Students work through the list in pairs before feeding back to the rest of the class.

Working with words

Extra activity

Ask students to close their books. Then read out the following percentages and ask students to write them down.

87%   78%   66%   62%   51%   8%   58%   55%   46% 32%   30%

Students then open their books and scan the text to find out what each percentage refers to.

Watch out! Students familiar with American English will be used to the word *traveller* being spelt with one *l*, i.e. *traveler*.

1 Students read the text and answer the questions. They can then discuss their answers with a partner.

> **Answers**
> 1 Overall, business travellers seem to be more positive than negative about business travel, with 78% saying they enjoy it, although many business travellers also point out the obvious drawbacks of being away from home (55% say it affects their personal life).
> 2 Answers will vary.

Watch out! The text refers to '*virtual*' meetings. Check students understand that these are video conferences, in other words, participants talking to each other through cameras and video screens. Also be prepared to explain the following word in the text: *appreciate* = to recognize the benefits or importance of something.

2 **25, 26▷** Students might need to listen to the interviews twice in order to make notes in the table. Note that they might not understand certain words in the listening. These will be dealt with in the exercises which follow.

Answers

	Traveller 1	Traveller 2
Reason for visit	research trip (to find somewhere for a conference)	a trade exhibition
Where they are staying	The Patio	Hotel Doña María
Plans (professional / personal)	– find out about venues and entertainment – excursion to Cordoba – try some local specialities – do some shopping / buy souvenirs	– meet colleagues – look round the old town – have a meal

3 25▷ You could ask stronger students to match the words and definitions before listening.

Answers

1 s<u>igh</u>tseeing	6 spec<u>ia</u>lity
2 c<u>o</u>nference	7 n<u>igh</u>tlife
3 v<u>e</u>nue	8 exhib<u>i</u>tion
4 fac<u>i</u>lities	9 exc<u>u</u>rsion
5 hospit<u>a</u>lity	10 enter<u>tai</u>nment

Pronunciation

Afterwards, students can mark the word stress (marked on the answers above) on each word.

4 You could add a competitive element by allowing students to score points for correct guesses.

5 26▷ Before listening you could ask students to guess which words in A match with words in B. They then match the phrases to the pictures to confirm the meaning.

Answers

a meet up with	e drop (someone) off
b check in	f show (someone) around
c freshen up	g eat out
d pick (someone) up	h look around

Watch out! These phrases are multi-word verbs. Students may ask about the use of the object in these verbs. They fall into the following four categories:

- verbs which do not need an object – *check in, freshen up, eat out, go out, look around*
- verbs which can only be followed by an object – *meet up with someone*
- verbs which can only be split by the object – *show someone around*
- verbs which can be split or followed by an object – *pick someone up, pick up someone, drop someone off, drop off someone.*

Dictionary skills

It will be helpful to refer students to good dictionaries during these exercises so that they can use the information provided on multi-word verbs and word order.

Tip Refer students to the *Tip* about *travel*, *trip*, and *journey*.

>> If students need more practice, go to **Practice file 6** on page 112 of the **Student's Book**.

6 Students work in pairs. Allow about ten minutes for pairs to decide on their plan for the two visitors. One student should be in charge of taking notes on the final plan. Note that there is no correct answer. At the end each pair can present their plan to the class or compare it with another pair.

Feedback focus

Focus on the correct use and pronunciation of the nouns and verbs taught in this section. Note in particular the accurate use of any multi-word verbs.

Extra activity

Either in class or for homework, students could write an email to one (or both) of the two visitors in which they confirm arrangements for their visit.

ⓘ Refer students to the **Interactive Workbook Glossary** for further study.

Business communication skills

1 Discuss these lead-in questions as a class.

Pre-work learners

Ask students to work in small groups and imagine that someone is coming to visit their place of study (school or college). What would they show the visitor? What wouldn't they show?

2 27▷ Students listen and complete the agenda. They then compare it with a partner.

> **Answers**
> **Morning:** tour of facility with Aruna Singh.
> **Lunchtime:** meet Jacinta and Dilip Patel for lunch.
> **Afternoon:** meet the team.

3 27▷ Before listening again, you could ask students to predict the missing words.

> **Answers**
>
> | | |
> |---|---|
> | 1 Welcome to | 7 run through |
> | 2 finally meet you | 8 thought you could |
> | 3 your journey | 9 we'll catch up again |
> | 4 any trouble | 10 you'll get a chance |
> | 5 let me take | 11 Make sure |
> | 6 get you | 12 don't worry about |

Watch out! In the *Working with words* section students met a number of new multi-word verbs and this exercise introduces two more:
run through = talk through (an agenda / schedule)
catch up = meet / find out what has happened since the last meeting.

Extra activity

Before **4**, ask students to study the expressions in sentences 1–8 and to think of their own possible responses as the guest to each one.

4 Students match the responses.

> **Answers**
>
> | | | | |
> |---|---|---|---|
> | a | 2 | e | 6 |
> | b | 1 | f | 5 |
> | c | 7 / 8 | g | 4 |
> | d | 7 / 8 | h | 3 |

Extra activity

27▷ Play the listening again and ask students to listen and write down Marvin's responses to phrases 1–6 (they are not exactly the same as in **4**).
  Answers
  1 *Thank you. It's nice to be here.*
  2 *Likewise.*
  3 *It was fine, there was quite a lot of traffic.*
  4 *No, not at all, your directions were excellent.*
  5 *That's OK, I'll hang on to it if you don't mind.*
  6 *A coffee sounds nice.*

5 Students work in pairs and use the flow chart to role-play a dialogue similar to the one in the listening. With weaker classes you might need to talk through each part of the flow chart and elicit the type of phrases to be used.

6 After the first conversation, students can change roles and repeat the dialogue so that they both have a chance to be the visitor and host.

7 28▷ Students now listen to a slightly more formal way of welcoming groups of guests.

> **Answers**
> 1 Head of Public Relations
> 2 a guided tour in the morning and then a chance to meet the engineers over lunch
> 3 stay with Aruna at all times for their safety

8 28▷ Note that students are not completing expressions here, but are listening for more formal (and much longer) equivalents. You may need to play the listening twice to help students write down all the words they hear.

> **Answers**
> 1 On behalf of … it gives me great pleasure to welcome you to …
> 2 You will have the opportunity to …
> 3 Can I remind you that …
> 4 Please be sure to …

» If students need more practice, go to **Practice file 6** on page 112 of the **Student's Book**. Students might need to refer to the *Key expressions*.

9 Students use the phrases they wrote down in **8** to make a short, but formal welcome speech. Once the group has prepared their speech, each student should practise saying it to the rest of their group.

Feedback focus

Focus on the levels of formality in the language used in **8** and **9**. As part of your feedback, write down any expressions you hear which are inappropriate in terms of formality, and any good expressions. Afterwards, read the expressions out and ask the class to tell you if each expression is an example of formal or less formal language and whether it needs any improvement. Make sure that students understand when to use more / less formal language (e.g. more formal when speaking in public).

Tip Refer students to the *Tip* about *catch up*.

ⓘ Refer students to the **Interactive Workbook Email** and **Phrasebank** sections for further study.

Practically speaking

1 Discuss the four phrases as a class and decide how formal each one is.

> **Suggested answers**
> *Would you like a drink?* is clearly the most formal and polite.
> *Do you want a drink?* sounds quite informal and could almost be considered impolite in certain contexts.
> *Do you fancy a drink?* is also less formal but would be acceptable in many contexts.
> *Can I get you a drink?* is fairly neutral and can be used safely in most situations.

Watch out! You may have to explain the use of *fancy* in 3. Note in this context that it simply means the same as *Would you like …?*

2 29▷ Students complete the responses and then listen to check their answers.

> **Answers**
> | | | | |
> |---|---|---|---|
> | 1 | fine | 4 | sounds |
> | 2 | would | 5 | love |
> | 3 | please | 6 | time |

3 When setting this activity up, refer students back to the discussion of formality in **1**. Point out, for example, that *Would you like a …?* is the most likely expression to be used with a guest you don't know. If you have time, students can carry out all four role-plays, taking turns to be each of the four people.

Feedback focus

As the role-plays are quite short, give immediate feedback after each one. Make sure students are using appropriate expressions for offering, according to their role.

Language at work

Watch out! The context for this next section is a *clean room*. Although it isn't crucial to students' understanding of the language, they will probably be interested in the following background information.

> *Clean rooms are used by companies that produce microchips. The rooms are kept incredibly clean and large air filtration systems change the air about ten times a minute. This reduces the risk of particles in the air damaging the chips. Staff who work in the clean rooms have to wear bunny suits so that any particles from their bodies cannot come into contact with the chips.*

1 30▷ Students listen and answer the questions.

> **Answers**
> 1 it is where they assemble the units
> 2 dust
> 3 **a** clothing must be made from synthetic materials (no wool or cotton because natural fibres produce particles)
> **b** no jewellery can be worn

2 30▷ Students categorize items from the listening.

> **Answers**
> **necessary**
> room is dust-free, special overalls (bunny suits), clothes made of synthetic materials, helmet and air filter mask, strict procedure for putting on bunny suits
> **not necessary**
> getting undressed
> **against the rules**
> clothes made of natural fibres, wearing jewellery or watches

3 Students categorize the sentences.

> **Answers**
> | | | | |
> |---|---|---|---|
> | 1 | e | 4 | h |
> | 2 | a, g | 5 | b |
> | 3 | c, d | 6 | f |

Tip Refer students to the *Tip* about *supposed to*. Draw attention to sentence *f*. It is not as strong as the prohibition in sentence *e* because it is 'softened'.

≫ If students need more practice, go to **Practice file 6** on page 113 of the **Student's Book**.

4 Students work in pairs and prepare sentences to describe obligation and necessity where they work.

Pre-work learners

Ask students to complete the sentences about any of the following:
- their place of study
- their home (and perhaps their parents' rules)
- rules for their country (*e.g. in my country we have to drive on the right …*).

---

5 Students might be able to base some of their rules on a real place of work, but they will also need to create some information. One way to help students prepare is to ask pairs to draw up a list of imaginary rules for each item.

Students can then change partners and use their list to complete the role-play.

Feedback focus

While monitoring, check that students are using the verb forms correctly. Typical confusion may occur with *mustn't* and *don't have to*.

(i) Refer students to the **Interactive Workbook Exercises** and **Tests** for revision.

Case study

Background

The topic of this *Case study* is an intercultural problem and the reading text presents a real and highly sensitive situation in which the northern European temperament of the Swedish is contrasted with that of people in India. Potentially, such a topic is open to stereotyping and wide generalizations. However, the context is authentic and so will offer students the chance to comment on the issue and perhaps give examples of cross-cultural difficulties they have experienced. One way to lead into this area is to ask students how they think other nationalities view them. For example, the British are often described as *cold* and *reserved*. By asking students to begin by reflecting on how others see them generally makes it easier to comment on such issues. The context for the *Task* is a similar situation and encourages students to find solutions to such problems.

Allow a few minutes for students to read the text and be prepared to answer any questions about vocabulary.

Discussion

1 Students could list the problems in pairs and then discuss the first question as a class.

> **Possible answers**
> **Problems**
> • project is behind schedule
> • relationships between managers and teams is getting worse
> • meetings are long and outcomes are unclear
> • communication problems
> • different attitudes
>
> **Reasons**
> From the reading we should understand that there isn't a problem with the standard of work, so the issues must be due to cultural differences. For example, one side is taking longer to arrive at final decisions and the end conclusions are not

being defined. There is clearly a language problem – this is probably due to different accents and maybe some differences in their 'Englishes'. It is possible that the Indians have a more relaxed attitude to time and deadlines, whereas the Swedes are not being direct enough in their use of language.

2 Again, discuss this question as a class.

> **Possible answer**
> AKA could provide intercultural training to both sides. This would raise awareness of the cultural differences between the two nationalities and would encourage the people involved to see situations from the other culture's perspective. This should lead to a better working relationship.

3 Students can discuss this question in pairs. Answers will vary.

> **Possible answers**
> • find out as much as possible about the country's culture
> • attend intercultural training courses
> • learn the local language
> • speak to other people who have relocated to that country and find out about their experiences

4 If your students all work for the same company / come from the same country, you can discuss this as a class. If the students are from different companies / countries, they can discuss in pairs before feeding back to the rest of the class.

Task

1 Students work in pairs. Allow time for them to read the *Files* and make a list of the issues.

2 Students discuss their list of issues in pairs.

3 Students now need to discuss the listed suggestions, before presenting their chosen solution to another group. Feedback should focus on effective communication of information and clear presentations of a proposed solution.

One-to-one

Follow the *Case study* as given. When you get to the *Task* the student can play the role of Student A and you can take the role of Student B.

» **Unit 6 Progress test** and **Speaking test**, pages 96–97.

Unit content

By the end of this unit, students will be able to
- talk about security measures and security breaches in the workplace
- explain and ask about changes
- introduce and respond to news by creating and showing interest
- use the present perfect simple, present perfect continuous, and connectors for talking about change and consequences.

Context

Security has become one of the most talked about issues in business. It concerns companies at all levels. Visitors who arrive at reception will need an identity badge. Computer networks need to constantly update software to protect company secrets from hackers or to guard against computer viruses. Furthermore, security services themselves have become hugely profitable businesses.

All your students (in-work or pre-work) will have experience of dealing with security in one form or another. In-work learners will be familiar with the need to follow security or safety requirements when visiting a company. They may have even attended meetings to discuss the need for improved security.

'Change' is another key theme in this unit and is a concept that is relevant to all modern businesses. Faster technology means that change is constant and usually at high speed. Change also needs to be managed so that everyone knows what is happening and how best to adjust to it. The language for understanding and explaining change is presented in the unit. Students will also have the opportunity to discuss a variety of issues relating to security, including the problem of data theft, which is the focus of the *Case study*.

Starting point

Students can discuss the questions in pairs or as a class.

Extension

Write the following discussion questions on the board.
- *Do you think all the security measures at work are necessary?*
- *Would you introduce any more measures?*

Students can discuss in pairs before feeding back to the rest of the class.

Working with words

Alternative

As an alternative to **1**, ask students to work in pairs. Student A works with the first text and Student B with the second text. Ask students to write three questions about their text. They can then swap their questions with a partner, who checks them and finds the answers.

1 Give students a time limit (one to two minutes) to find the answers to the questions.

Watch out! You might need to pre-teach the following:
breach = an action that breaks a rule or agreement.

> **Answers**
> 1 In the first reading the security breach was theft of information from databases as a result of unauthorized access. In the second, the employee stole in full view of security cameras.
> 2 Personal information was stolen in the first case; DVDs and CDs were stolen in the second case.
> 3 A credit agency and its customers in the first case; the company where the thief was employed in the second case.

Tip Refer students to the *Tip* about *safety* and *security*.

2 Allow a few minutes for students to find the words.

> **Answers**
>
> | Security measures | Security breaches |
> | --- | --- |
> | password | unauthorized access |
> | security pass | identify theft |
> | security cameras | stealing |
> | security staff | entering a system without passwords |
> | monitor | |

3 Students discuss these questions in pairs and then summarize their discussion for the whole class.

Pre-work learners

Students discuss the same three questions, but about their place of study. For example:

Has there ever been a security breach at your place of study?

4 Students look for the verbs to complete the combinations.

> **Answers**
> 1 safeguard
> 2 deter
> 3 monitor

Explain to students that many other verbs are followed by particular prepositions and that it is useful to record this information when learning a new verb.

Extra activity

Ask students to look back at the two texts and find further verb + preposition combinations. The texts include the following:

> *notified of, gained (access) to, arrest (someone) for, stealing from, open up.*

⏵⏵ If students need more practice, go to **Practice file 7** on page 114 of the **Student's Book**.

5 Students complete the sentences.

> **Answers**
> 1 insure … against
> 2 prevent … from / stop … from
> 3 check … for / scan … for
> 4 prevent … from / stop … from / deter …from
> 5 safeguard against / protect against
> 6 check … for / monitor … for / scan … for

6 Allow students time to think of their definitions and make sure they are using the verb + preposition combinations in **4**.

> **Possible answers**
> protects against worms and hackers (anti-virus software)
> deters burglars from breaking in (CCTV)
> stops someone from logging in to private data (password)
> insures against unauthorized entry (security pass)
> scans for illegal objects (X-ray machine)
> safeguards against thieves (burglar alarm)
> prevents someone from opening a lock (lock and key)

Students could then think of their own security measures and describe what they are for so that their partner can guess. Other measures might include: *body searches, checking DNA, taking fingerprints, checking passports, walls and fences, turnstiles, alarms,* or *guard dogs.*

7 Students need to think back to the discussions in the *Starting point* and give reasons for the security measures.

Feedback focus

Focus on the correct use of word combinations from **4**.

Extra activity

Ask students to think of a building they know well. It could be one of the following: a building at work, a school / college building, the local train station. Students work in pairs and imagine that they own a security consultancy firm and have been asked to provide security measures for the building. Pairs make lists of measures and reasons for needing them. At the end, they report back to the rest of the class.

ⓘ Refer students to the **Interactive Workbook Glossary** for further study.

Business communication skills

1 You might need to discuss the advantages and disadvantages for the first security measure as a class. You could write the following table on the board.

Swipe card

(+)	(−)
can contain lots of information	easily stolen or lost
easy to carry	eventually needs replacing
can be updated	if the system breaks down it will cause a lot of problems
does not require people	

Students can then work in pairs and think of advantages and disadvantages for the other three measures. Then ask pairs for their ideas and write them on the board.

> **Some possible answers**
> **ID card**
> + easy to make, easy to check by photo
> – can be forged, easy to lose, must be checked by people
> **PIN number**
> + very secure, can be changed quickly, can be combined with swipe card for extra security
> – easy to forget, someone might steal it by watching
> **Key**
> + cheap, small
> – easy to lose, steal, or copy

2 **31▷** Students listen and answer the questions.

> **Answers**
> 1 current system is identity badges, new system is swipe cards
> 2 the advantage is that every person's ID can be checked, the disadvantage is that staff will have to swipe every time they go through a door

Extra activity

Write the following statements on the board. Students listen and decide if they are true (T) or false (F) (answers given in brackets).
> 1 *People have breached security to get into the building. (T)*
> 2 *Staff have lost personal items. (F)*
> 3 *The electronic boxes will be installed at the end of the month. (F)*
> 4 *Security staff are being lazy and aren't doing their job properly. (F)*
> 5 *You don't need a PIN number with the cards. (T)*

3 **31▷** Students match and then listen to check their answers.

> **Answers**
> | 1 | f | 7 | l |
> |---|---|---|---|
> | 2 | h | 8 | c |
> | 3 | e | 9 | j |
> | 4 | d | 10 | a |
> | 5 | b | 11 | i |
> | 6 | g | 12 | k |

4 When students have categorized the phrases, they can check their answers by referring to the *Key expressions* list.

> **Answers**
> a 1, 2, 6
> b 3, 4, 12
> c 8, 10, 11
> d 5, 7, 9

>> If students need more practice, go to **Practice file 7** on page 114 of the **Student's Book**. Students might need to refer to the *Key expressions*.

5 Students begin by working alone. Allow students time to make notes from their *Files*. Advise them to make notes under two headings – *Current situation* and *Changes*. You could put Student As together and Student Bs together to help them prepare for the speaking activity. Their notes should include the following information.

> **Student A notes**
> **Current situation**
> – problems with underground car park
> – employee's bag stolen
> **Changes**
> – install CCTV in car park and corridors by the end of the month
> – these are connected to screens in reception

> **Student B notes**
> **Current situation**
> – problems with virus on the network
> – hacker tried to read employee information
> **Changes**
> – install new software to scan computers
> – start new system of passwords
> – new password every month from department manager

Students then work in pairs and take turns to present and justify their changes. Refer students to the *Key expressions* list to help them. Encourage Student B to ask for clarification and explanation. They must be satisfied that A's reasons for change are good enough.

One-to-one

For **5**, you can follow the same procedure, with you and the student taking turns to be A or B. Alternatively, ask the student to complete notes on both emails and imagine that both sets of changes are taking place in the same company.

6 Allow plenty of time for students to think and make notes about a change at work. When students present the changes to a partner or group make sure they use language from the *Key expressions*.

Pre-work learners

Students can present a change at their school or college, or create an imaginary new system of security for their place of study. Alternatively, they could think of a system in their country that has changed (e.g. airport security).

Feedback focus

Focus on correct use of expressions, but also be prepared to help with language to describe security measures and descriptions of procedures. Note that some students may try to use the passive form. This is dealt with in detail in *Unit 14* so you might not want to correct this too much at this stage.

>> Refer students to the **Interactive Workbook Email** and **Phrasebank** sections for further study.

Practically speaking

1 Students categorize the phrases. Point out to students that these phrases not only help to create interest in what you are saying, but they also encourage active listening resulting in more fulfilling conversations.

2 32▷ Students listen to the phrases in context and check their ideas.

Answers			
1 S		5 C	
2 S		6 S	
3 C		7 S	
4 C		8 S	

3 This simple, but fun activity allows students to try out the expressions. Allow a few minutes for students to think of true and false news. You could demonstrate the activity by telling the class about some of your news and letting them guess if it's true or not.

Language at work

1 As a lead-in, you could begin by brainstorming the structure of these tenses with the class and writing them on the board. Alternatively you could write sentences 5 and 6 from the previous *Practically speaking* section on the board and draw attention to the form as follows.

to have + past participle
*I've just **heard** about something really interesting.*
*I've never **heard** that before.*

If students seem unfamiliar with the forms you might want to refer them to *Practice file 7* on page 115 of the *Student's Book* and ask them to complete the exercises there before continuing.

Answers	
1 a	2 b

2 Even though students might be less comfortable with the present perfect continuous at this level, recognizing the form shouldn't create too much difficulty.

Answers
present perfect simple: b
present perfect continuous: a

» If students need more practice, go to **Practice file 7** on page 115 of the **Student's Book**.

3 If students find it hard to decide, refer them to the language reference section in *Practice file 7*.

Answers
1 '␣ve been working	3 met
2 '␣ve completed	4 '␣ve understood

Watch out! Draw student's attention to question 4. *Understood* is a state verb, (such as *like* and *be*) and so usually appears in the simple form, regardless of the situation.

4 This is primarily a speaking activity. However, if you feel students are still having difficulty with the forms, they could begin by writing out the questions. Make sure students use either the present perfect simple or the present perfect continuous.

5 Students read the sentences and answer the questions. They can then compare their answers with a partner. These sentences include connectors, which are used for explaining reasons for actions. The connectors are especially useful for explaining change.

Answers
1 result
2 reason
3 reason
4 reason

6 These connectors have the same function as some of the connectors in the sentences in **5**.

Answers
1 Consequently = so / therefore / as a result
2 In order that = so that
3 because of = due to
4 in order to = to

» If students need more practice, go to **Practice file 7** on page 115 of the **Student's Book**.

7 Students use the words given to help form sentences with the present perfect simple or present perfect continuous. They should also try to add a connector to explain the reason for what has happened / been happening.

Pre-work learners

Students can make sentences about what has been happening in their life in general. You could give a personal example to help start this off. For example:

I've recently been leaving home early to get to work, because of the traffic.

Feedback focus

This speaking task is fairly challenging, so allow a few minutes for students to experiment before correcting sentences.

ⓘ Refer students to the **Interactive Workbook Exercises** and **Tests** for revision.

Case study

Background

This *Case study* presents a real example of a security breach. Students are encouraged to consider the effects of this incident on both the customers and the company involved. They also have to think about how future security breaches could be avoided. The concept of preventing security problems provides the context for the *Task*, where students have to discuss a company's security options and then use the language from the unit to present their ideas.

Allow time for students to read the text and be prepared to answer any questions about vocabulary.

Discussion

1–3 Students discuss the questions in pairs. Encourage them to make notes on their discussion so that they can report back to the rest of the class.

> **Possible answers**
> 1 The bad publicity for the security firm may mean that customers lose confidence in it and take their business elsewhere.
> 2 The company could write a letter to all of its customers and assure them of the security measures being used and any changes that are being made.
> 3 The company could
> – change its passwords more regularly
> – issue passwords to fewer people.

Task

1 Students work in groups of three or four. Allow plenty of time for students to read and understand the listed options.

2 Suggest that one student takes notes on the discussion by writing the advantages and disadvantages for each option as shown in the following box. Then ask students to choose their three most important options.

Possible answers

	Advantages	Disadvantages
1	you could know about all the staff	very time consuming
2	limits information leaving the building	we need employees to be able to work from home
3	this would mean there are fewer staff to check (in 1)	it might be inconvenient to limit the numbers
4	limits information leaving the building	USB devices are more convenient than using laptops
5	makes sure everyone is aware of the situation and requirements	time consuming
6	would improve morale and stability	expensive and suggests you can't trust employees
7	the information is centralized and controlled	impractical, inconvenient, and still means data can be accessed externally
8	will stop anyone without the password	people always forget passwords

3 Groups get together and present their ideas. In order to agree on a final action plan, students will need to refer back to their ideas in **2**. Feedback should focus on the effectiveness of the discussion and the use of expressions when presenting ideas for making a change.

One-to-one

Follow the *Case study* as given and then discuss the options together. The student could then prepare and give a presentation of the ideas.

» **Unit 7 Progress test** and **Speaking test**, pages 98–99.

Unit content

By the end of this unit, students will be able to
- talk about teamwork
- present and discuss plans
- give encouragement
- use *will*, *going to*, and modals for talking about goals.

Context

The topic of *Working together*, either in a team or in a partnership, is relevant to most business people today. In many cases, teams are made up of people of different nationalities, with English being the common language. These teams may involve people from the same international company, or they could involve freelance staff and external consultants.

In recent years, businesses have focused on how to create effective teams and partnerships. The aim is to bring individuals together whose personal skills and knowledge can help the team to achieve a common goal. Companies might ask employees to attend training courses or complete questionnaires in order to develop their teamwork skills or identify who will work best together. Effective teamwork not only results in better company performance, but also improves employee morale and makes the individual feel valued.

It's important to remember that teams may encounter problems. If the team contains a number of strong personalities, there may be conflict. International teams can also encounter difficulties if members have different perspectives on teamwork. Some cultures value the success of individuals, whilst other cultures consider collaborative work to be more important, and these differing attitudes could lead to misunderstandings. In reaction to these potential problems, the focus for team managers has shifted from being the expert, to being the person who 'manages' different talents and temperaments, and makes sure that the team works as one.

This unit presents the language students need in order to build effective teams and to participate effectively in team meetings. There are also many opportunities for students to describe their own experiences of teamwork.

Starting point

Allow time for students to match the partnerships. They can then compare their answers with a partner and discuss 2 and 3 together. Question 4 can then be discussed as a class.

Answers

John Lennon and Paul McCartney
They were the songwriting partnership in The Beatles and worked in the music industry. Although they always signed their songs as Lennon and McCartney, they reportedly wrote many of the later songs separately and took input from each other. They inspired each other through the competitive nature of their partnership.

Domenico Dolce and Stefano Gabbana
Dolce and Gabbana is a famous Italian brand in the fashion industry which was set up by two young designers.

Philips and Douwe Egberts
Philips makes electronic household goods and Douwe Egberts produces coffee. The two companies have collaborated to produce coffee machines which use easy-to-use coffee capsules.

Crédit Lyonnais and Tour de France
Crédit Lyonnais is a French bank which has sponsored the Tour de France cycling race for a number of years. The famous yellow jersey worn by Tour de France champions also shows the name Crédit Lyonnais.

Working with words

1 Discuss this question as a class. Students' responses may vary, but the key point to make is that each person needs to be able to work well in a team.

2 Again, discuss this as a class. Note that responses will depend on job types and roles within a company. Extend the discussion by asking students if they think time spent working with others and in meetings is useful.

Pre-work learners

Ask your students to think about when they have been involved in a team, e.g. a sports team at school or a group project at college. As a result of this experience what do they think makes a successful team?

3 This quiz is typical of the type of tests which assess your ability to work in a team. Students can compare their answers and discuss whether they would be good team players.

Watch out! You might need to pre-teach the following:
rivals = people (or companies / teams) who often compete
to get on with someone = to like someone and have a good relationship with them.

Encourage students to interpret responses to the statements and decide what response would show that someone would work well in a team and what response might show that someone would work better independently. There are no right or wrong answers, but it will prepare students for the next listening exercise.

4 33▷ Students listen and complete the questionnaire for the candidate.

Answers

1	Disagree	**4**	Agree
2	Agree	**5**	Agree
3	Agree	**6**	Agree

5 33▷ Students match the words to make various collocations before listening to check.

Answers

take responsibility	common ground
team player	form alliances
work closely	joint venture
join forces	mutual benefit
complementary skills	shared goals

Pronunciation

The following words may cause difficulty, so read them aloud and ask students to mark the word stress. You can then quickly drill them.

responsi<u>bi</u>lity, comple<u>men</u>tary, al<u>li</u>ances, <u>bene</u>fit, <u>mutu</u>al

6 Students now check their understanding of the phrases in **5**.

Answers

1	complementary skills	**6**	work closely
2	join forces	**7**	joint venture
3	take responsibility	**8**	shared goals
4	mutual benefit	**9**	team player
5	form alliances	**10**	common ground

Extra activity

For more practice with the new vocabulary you could ask students to do two things.

1 Student A closes his / her book and Student B reads out the definitions in **6**. Students A tries to remember the correct phrase.

2 Students work in pairs and write ten sentences or a short paragraph using the phrases in a context that is relevant to their work, studies, or life. For example:
I take responsibility for any mistakes my team make.

» If students need more practice, go to **Practice file 8** on page 116 of the **Student's Book**.

Tip Refer students to the *Tip* about *rather*.

7 Ask students to list their own strengths and weaknesses in order to help them decide who they will need to join the team. Emphasize that the team needs to involve a good balance of people who have complementary skills. Each pair should then present their choices to the class with a short explanation for their choices.

Feedback focus

Focus on correct use and pronunciation of the phrases in **5**.

Alternative

If your students are not involved in projects, or you would like to offer them alternatives, write the following project descriptions on the board:

* *producing a company newsletter to be published four times a year*
* *analysing how your department could reduce its costs and producing an action plan*
* *investigating and planning an open day at your company, when people living locally can visit and look round.*

Students can work in pairs and choose a project. They then follow the procedure in **7**. If you have extra time, students could create teams for each project.

ⓘ Refer students to the **Interactive Workbook Glossary** for further study.

Business communication skills

1 During this discussion, the topic of company culture may arise. For example, some companies have a culture which is quite closed and people work alone, whereas others have more of an open-door policy. Company culture is a key issue in joint ventures between two different companies and will affect the response to each of the four areas listed.

2 34▷ Before listening, briefly discuss with the class why there might be feelings of suspicion between staff. For example, some staff may feel that there is a danger of staff cuts and redundancies if new people arrive.

Watch out! You might need to pre-teach the following:
two-camps mentality = two sides or groups of people and an attitude towards the other side which may be negative or suspicious
inevitable = impossible to prevent.

Answers
Nikos's plan: hold a series of informal meetings for staff.
How it will work: people can meet informally and develop a relationship.
Timescale of plan: seven or eight meetings by the end of next month.
What he needs before he can launch it: a list of Buckler's key people.

3 If necessary, play the listening again to help students answer this question.

Answer
a big event which will be fun – Carmen wants ideas on this

4 34▷ With stronger classes, you could ask students to predict the missing words before listening.

Answers

1	expect	8	By
2	leave	9	step
3	Over	10	likely
4	plan	11	term
5	take	12	chances
6	intend	13	long
7	timescale		

Tip Refer students to the *Tip*. Ask students to say one thing that they think is *likely* to happen this week and what they are *pretty* sure will happen this week.

5 Students categorize the phrases.

Answers
a   1, 4, 6, 10, 11, 12, 13
b   3, 5, 7, 8
c   2, 9

» If students need more practice, go to **Practice file 8** on page 116 of the **Student's Book**. Students might need to refer to the *Key expressions*.

6 Allow plenty of time for students to study their information. Monitor and help with any unknown vocabulary. Each student will need to begin by presenting their plans and intentions. Make sure that students use the phrases from this section. Refer them to the *Key expressions* to help them.

7 Students work alone and plan the next twelve months. If necessary they can make up information. They can present their plans to the whole class or to groups of four or five if the class is large.

Feedback focus

As well as giving feedback on the phrases, a number of time prepositions will arise in this activity (see the last section in the *Key expressions*), so you may wish to focus on this area of language.

ⓘ Refer students to the **Interactive Workbook Email** and **Phrasebank** sections for further study.

Practically speaking

1 35▷ The language point here is quite subtle and won't be obvious to some students. The speaker in *b* and *e* isn't saying something is bad, but isn't giving it 100% support.

Answers
1   a, c, d
2   b, e

2 Students work in groups. One student should note down the ideas.

Pre-work learners

Students could come up with an idea to improve their place of study or they could design an advert with a slogan to encourage people to study there.

3 Groups present their creations or ideas and other students comment on them, using phrases in **1**.

Language at work

1 As a lead-in, ask students to try and remember the reasons for the meeting in the *Business communication skills* section. Elicit the fact that two companies were merging and managers were considering ways to bring new members of staff together. Explain that the email from Carmen follows on from that meeting.

Students read and answer 1–2 on their own. They can then compare their answers with a partner.

Answers
1   She is optimistic about the schedule and thinks that they should be in the new premises by the end of June as planned.
2   She predicts that there could be trouble and some people will leave because of the changes.

Tip Refer students to the *Tip* about *by the way* and *incidentally*.

2 Students complete the rules.

> **Answers**
> 1 'll / will   4 should
> 2 could / might 5 going to
> 3 going to   6 'll / will

3 Students now complete the sentences using the words in **2**.

> **Answers**
> a should   d might / could
> b will   e going to
> c ll   f going to

» If students need more practice, go to **Practice file 8** on page 117 of the **Student's Book**.

4 The verb forms that students choose for their sentences may vary.

> **Possible answers**
> 1 I'm going to finish on time.
> 2 She should be here in fifteen minutes.
> 3 We might not reach our targets if sales don't improve.
> 4 I might apply for the job.
> 5 It'll be there in two days.

5 Responses will vary, according to students' goals.

Feedback focus

Distinguishing between future forms is difficult for students to do in an output task, and *will* and *going to* can often be used interchangeably. Focus your feedback on any obvious mistakes. The main aim is for students to consciously practise future forms.

ⓘ Refer students to the **Interactive Workbook Exercises** and **Tests** for revision.

Case study

Background

This *Case study* presents a real example of a company that uses virtual teamworking (using the Internet and conference calls to meet their colleagues). Students are encouraged to think about the advantages and disadvantages of this concept. The *Task* allows students to think about the best teamwork solutions for an international company. They discuss and present their ideas, using language presented in the unit.

With an in-work class, ask students what kind of technology they use to communicate at their place of work. Briefly discuss their experiences of using these methods of communication before asking students to read the text.

Discussion

1–3 Students discuss the questions in pairs before feeding back to the rest of the class. You could write their answers on the board. Note that during the *Task* they will read a comprehensive list detailing the advantages and disadvantages of virtual teamwork, so their initial ideas for questions **2** and **3** can be compared with this list at the *Task* stage.

> **Possible answer**
> 1 a group of people who work together, but who are located in different places and 'meet' using their PCs

Task

1 Students read about the company and the various events. Note that some events are more suitable for virtual meetings than others. For example, general conferences only happen once every two years and include a *social event*, so a virtual meeting in this case may be inappropriate.

2 You then need to divide into As and Bs. Put As together and Bs together so that they can read through their information, make notes, and check with each other that they have understood.

3 Regroup the students so that As mix with Bs. Students discuss their *Files* and summarize the advantages and disadvantages. They then begin a full discussion of their plans for the five events.

4 End with presentations from each group. Feedback should focus on how effectively students were able to discuss and present their plans.

One-to-one

Work together on the *Case study* with your student. However, instead of splitting the two *Files*, let your student study both the list of advantages and disadvantages. Discuss with your student what changes they would make to the events.

» **Unit 8 Progress test** and **Speaking test**, pages 100–101.

Logistics

Unit content

By the end of this unit, students will be able to
- talk about logistics and supply chains
- place and handle orders
- leave voicemail messages
- use reported speech for talking about problems and disagreements.

Context

The topic of *Logistics* will have relevance at different levels for your students. Logistics refers to the effective organization of something that is complex. For your students this may mean involvement in the planning and streamlining of supply chains, or the organization of a product or service from its conception to its sale. Logistics is even relevant to home life. For example, a parent may have to get children up, make breakfast, get to school, and then to work.

Traditionally, logistics is concerned with the flow of goods from raw-material stage to manufacture and then transportation. Large manufacturing companies will have logistics departments which manage this process and ensure that everything arrives and leaves on time. There are also logistics companies, such as DHL, who operate internationally and have to find logistical solutions.

In recent years business has paid more attention to logistics. Improving the efficiency and speed of goods delivery often results in huge savings. With the growth of online shopping, more companies are also able to bypass the distributor and shop retailer, and deliver directly to the customer. This has brought about changes to traditional notions of supply and has increased the profits for many companies. Dell is a well-known example, and features in this unit.

The unit presents the language needed when talking about logistics, and prepares students to deal with any logistical problems that may arise. Students also have the opportunity to participate in role-plays which allow them to practise expressions for dealing with problematic orders.

Starting point

Students can discuss these questions in pairs before feeding back to the rest of the class. Refer to the *Context* for a definition of *logistics*.

Working with words

1 Discuss this question as a class.

2 As a lead-in, ask students what type of computers they use at work and at home. Then ask what your students already know about Dell. Allow a minute for students to read and find answers to the questions.

Watch out! You might need to pre-teach the following:
conventional = traditional / ordinary
appropriate = suitable, acceptable, or correct for the particular circumstances
by pass = avoid / go past.

> **Answers**
> 1 Dell does not have to keep raw materials or maintain stock levels in warehouses. It builds the product once it has the order. It advertises and delivers directly to customers and so doesn't need distributors and shopkeepers. It is also paid by customers before having to pay its suppliers, so there are no cash-flow problems.
> 2 Suppliers have to give credit to Dell, even though Dell has the money.

3 Students match the words to the definitions.

> **Answers**
> 1 retailers
> 2 inventory
> 3 warehouses
> 4 components
> 5 streamlined
> 6 supply chain
> 7 clients
> 8 distributors
> 9 suppliers
> 10 manufacturers
> 11 raw materials

Extension

One student reads out the definitions and the other student (with the book closed) guesses the word. You could also use this as an opportunity to check for correct pronunciation.

Extra activity

With a class of in-work students, ask them to tick any of the eleven words from the text which affect the type of business they are in. Students then work in pairs and explain the connection. For example:
In my business we store all our goods in warehouses before they go to the retailers.

Pronunciation

Read out the words and ask students to mark the stress.
re<u>tai</u>lers, <u>in</u>ventory, <u>ware</u>houses, com<u>po</u>nents, <u>stream</u>lined, sup<u>ply</u>, <u>cli</u>ents, dis<u>tri</u>butors, su<u>ppli</u>ers, manu<u>fac</u>turers, ma<u>te</u>rials

4 This activity encourages students to discuss and summarize the information in the text. Students put the words into the flowchart.

> **Answers**
> 1 supplier ➜ manufacturer ➜ distributor ➜ retailer ➜ customer
> 2 supplier ➜ manufacturer ➜ customer

5 36▷ Students listen and answer the questions.

> **Answers**
> 1 His business is tiny by comparison, but it is also much more personal. He can give more time to discussing customer needs and deals with any problems in the shop. He also has to keep lots of components in stock.
> 2 using bar codes and a database
> 3 by tracking them

6 36▷ Students listen and complete the phrases.

> **Answers**
> 1 in
> 2 out
> 3 on
> 4 out
> 5 out
> 6 on
> 7 up
> 8 keep

7 Students now match the phrases to the pictures.

> **Answers**
> a run low on
> b run out of
> c in stock
> d out of stock
> e stock up on

» If students need more practice, go to **Practice file 9** on page 118 of the **Student's Book**.

8 Students work in pairs and take turns to ask and answer the six questions. You could model the activity by answering some of the questions yourself.

9 Encourage students to use some of the phrases from the listening during this activity.

Pre-work learners

For the second question, students could describe the supply chain at a company they know well.

Feedback focus

Monitor for correct use and pronunciation of the vocabulary presented in this section.

Extra activity

If students know a lot about their company's supply chain, ask them to give a presentation to the class. They could draw a similar flowchart to those shown in **4** as a visual aid and talk everyone through it.

ⓘ Refer students to the **Interactive Workbook Glossary** for further study.

Business communication skills

1 As a lead-in, ask students if they know how office supplies are normally ordered in their companies. By phone? Fax? Email? Students can then read the email and answer questions 1–4.

Watch out! You might need to pre-teach the following:
motherboards = the main board of a computer, containing all the circuits
asap = an abbreviation commonly used in emails meaning as soon as possible.

> **Answers**
> 1 2,000 motherboards
> 2 yes (because she says it's a repeat order and to charge it to her account as usual)
> 3 as soon as possible
> 4 on account

2 Students underline any useful phrases that would help them write their own email to place an order.

> **Suggested answers**
> I would like to place an order for …
> We need these …
> … please send them asap
> Please charge it to our account …

Extra activity

Ask students to write their own email to place an order using the underlined expressions. Students can think of something they often order for work and write an email to the supplier. Alternatively, write the following notes for an order on the board and ask them to write the email:
- *20 screens, 25 keyboards*
- *needed by the 25th of next month.*

3 37▷ Students listen and complete the information.

Watch out! You may want to make the distinction between the following:
dispatched = something has been sent, but has not yet arrived
delivered = something has been sent and has arrived.

> **Answers**
> **Account reference**: PG 278
> **Date of order**: 11th February
> **Product description**: motherboards
> **Dispatched**: yes
> **Date and time dispatched**: 11th February, afternoon

4 37▷ Before students listen again they could try to predict the missing words in the phrases.

> **Answers**
> 1 following up
> 2 find out
> 3 account details
> 4 place
> 5 straight through
> 6 According to
> 7 must have
> 8 happy about
> 9 check it out
> 10 I'll look into it
> 11 real
> 12 as quick as
> 13 happened

>> If students need more practice, go to **Practice file 9** on page 118 of the **Student's Book**. Students might need to refer to the *Key expressions*.

Tip Refer students to the *Tip* about clarifying spelling and numbers.

Extra activity

Following on from the *Tip* and for further practice before the next exercise, ask students to write down the names of three famous people. They then spell those names to their partner, who writes them down. Make sure that they use a common word to illustrate each letter.

5 Begin by looking at the two sets of flow charts as a class. Elicit phrases students might use at each stage of the conversation. You could also ask students to match expressions from **4** to each part of the conversation and decide which will be useful. Students will then need a minute to read and understand their role in the *Files* before starting the conversations. Note that there are two different situations, so students take turns to be the call handler and customer. Refer students to the *Key expressions* list to help them.

Feedback focus

Focus on the use of expressions and techniques for clarifying the information. After feedback, students could change partners and repeat the role-plays. If there's time, some pairs could demonstrate their conversations to the rest of the class.

Extra activity

If your students often write emails you could repeat the role-plays in **5**, but rather than calling each other, students could simulate emails being sent from the customer to the supplier as follows.
  1 Student A looks at situation 1 (as the customer from an oil company) and writes an email to the supplier.
  2 Student B looks at situation 2 (as the customer from the fashion trade) and writes an email to Haddows Trading.
  3 Students swap their emails – they both become the relevant supplier in their *Files* (A looks at situation 2, B at situation 1) and write their response.
  4 They swap again and return to their roles as customers (continue like this until the situations are resolved by email).
Students will each need at least one blank sheet of paper. Alternatively, ask them to write some of the emails for homework. You can then collect their emails and provide feedback.

ⓘ Refer students to the **Interactive Workbook Email** and **Phrasebank** sections for further study.

Practically speaking

1 38▷ As a lead-in, ask your students what information they give on their voicemail recorded message. Elicit ideas such as name, number, where they are, what time to call back, when to leave a message. Students then listen for the instructions in each message.

> **Answers**
> 1 leave a message and a contact number
> 2 call back during office hours
> 3 hold

Extra activity

If your students need to record their own voicemails in English, ask them to turn to *Audio script 38* ▷ and underline any useful expressions from the three voicemails. They could also write out a voicemail recorded message using the expressions and you could ask them to read it aloud to the class.

2 Phrases a–h are for the caller to use when leaving a message.

> **Answers**
> 1 b, f,
> 2 e, g
> 3 a
> 4 c, d, h

3 39▷ Students order phrases 1–4 and then listen and check their ideas.

> **Answers**
> **First**: Identifying yourself (3)
> **Second**: Giving the time of your call (2)
> **Third**: Giving a reason for the call (4)
> **Fourth**: Leaving a contact number (1)

4 As students leave their messages, the other students can take notes on the key information.

Extra activity

Students can write their own message to leave on a voicemail and read it to a partner, who makes notes. The message could be the type of message they often have to leave for their work, or alternatively a message to a friend. If students created their own voicemail recorded messages earlier (see previous *Extra activity*), the first student could read this aloud before the caller leaves a message.

Language at work

1 40▷ As a lead-in, elicit from the class what had happened to Gisele's order from earlier in this unit and check they remember the essential information (she'd ordered 2,000 motherboards and there had been a delay with the delivery). Students then listen for the two pieces of information.

> **Answers**
> **Problem with order**: it was sent by sea not by international courier.
> **Solution**: to send 400 by courier immediately.

2 Sentences 1–4 all come from the listening and report what was said. Students write the direct speech. You could model the first answer on the board if necessary.

> **Answers**
> 1 Can you tell me what has happened to it?
> 2 It went two weeks ago.

3 We've sent it by sea.
4 Do you know where it is?

3 Students categorize the reported speech sentences.

> **Answers**
> 1 b, c   3 a
> 2 d   4 e

4 Students can complete these rules by checking the use of *say* and *tell* in sentences a–e.

> **Answers**
> 1 say
> 2 tell
> 3 say

Watch out! You may need to mention exceptions to the second rule: *tell a story / tell a joke*.

» If students need more practice, go to **Practice file 9** on page 119 of the **Student's Book**.

5 41▷ Students complete the message.

> **Answers**
> **Message from**: Linda
> **Time**: 3.30
> **Message**: Have sent 400 motherboards by courier.
> Linda told carrier this was top priority.
> Arriving in two days.
> **Reference / tracking number**: HA 9872367

6 Students work in pairs. The student who is Gisele should practise using reported speech by reporting Linda's message in **5**. Students can then change roles and repeat the activity.

Extra activity

Ask students to prepare a message that they would leave on someone's voicemail. They then read it to their partner, who takes notes. Afterwards, the listener has to report the message back. This means that the listener has to use reported speech and also ensures that he / she took the correct information.

7 Allow time for students to think of their problem. They might want to make notes to help them when telling the group. They will also need to think about what reported speech structures they intend to use.

Feedback focus

Using reported speech at this level will be challenging, so focus feedback on the accuracy of these structures, rather than on anything else.

ⓘ Refer students to the **Interactive Workbook Exercises** and **Tests** for revision.

Case study

Background

This *Case study* presents a real situation faced by Castorama Polska. Students have the opportunity to discuss the possible consequences of logistics problems and can compare their suggestions for changes with what actually happened in this case. The *Task* uses the context of logistics problems and enables students to practise the language presented in the unit.

Allow time for students to read the text and be prepared to answer any questions about vocabulary.

Discussion

1–5 Students can discuss the questions in small groups or as a class.

Possible answers
1 home improvement products (DIY)
2 Orders were delayed and customers were unhappy with the customer service.
 This happened because the company grew, but the logistics system was unable to cope with the large numbers of orders. Each store was a logistically independent unit which made it difficult to coordinate supply and demand.
3 • cuts out parts of the process (e.g. middlemen)
 • leads to faster delivery times
 • company can operate without warehouses
 • lower costs
 • higher sales
4 & 5 Students can make their own suggestions for **4** and then turn to the *File* in **5** to compare their ideas with what actually happened when Maersk helped Castorama.

Task

1 Students work in pairs. Allow time for them to read about the situation. They then turn to their *Files* and prepare to report their findings.

Alternative

If you think that your students might find it difficult to digest all the information and report back, you could ask pairs to read through both *Files* and match the corresponding comments together.

2 Students discuss the findings and decide on the six logistics problems.

Possible answers
1 Staff can't track the progress of an order.
2 Each store is responsible for dealing with suppliers and documentation of orders which individual managers don't have time for.
3 Delivery times are not reliable because of traffic and problems finding the stores.
4 Transportation costs are high.
5 Too much room for human error with stock control system.
6 Getting popular items direct from suppliers takes too long.

Students then discuss possible solutions to these problems.

3 Student present their solutions to another group. Feedback should focus on how clearly students report their findings, and on the effectiveness of the proposed solutions.

One-to-one

Follow the *Case study* as given. When you get to the *Task* the student can play the role of student A, and you can take the role of student B. The student can then prepare and give a presentation of the proposed solution.

>> **Unit 9 Progress test** and **Speaking test**, pages 102–103.

Unit content

By the end of this unit, students will be able to
- describe their place of work
- make suggestions, recommendations, and appropriate responses
- link ideas and reasons
- use countable and uncountable nouns with quantifiers for talking about facilities.

Context

The topic of *Facilities* affects all your students, although they may not have spent much time previously considering it. Facilities can refer to services or equipment available in a certain environment. The importance of our working environment and how it can affect our performance is now widely recognized. The traditional image of work places might be offices with people in enclosed cubicles, or factories with rows of people in assembly lines. However, modern work spaces are far more diverse and many of the old stereotypes no longer exist.

Facilities also vary from place to place and this unit offers students the opportunity to compare their work places. The unit also enables students to practise the language of suggesting and recommending so that they can operate effectively in meetings or brainstorming sessions. Note that the culture within a company or a country may affect students' reactions when being asked for opinions and suggestions. In some cultures students might wait to be invited to speak or offer an opinion, whereas in other cultures the expectation could be that you will interrupt if you want to say something. This may be something to explore in classes with students from widely different backgrounds.

Starting point

These questions encourage students to think about working environments and what makes them pleasant places to work in. Discuss the questions as a class and encourage students to explain why they would like to work in certain places / buildings and not in others.

Working with words

1 The text is about a car plant in Dresden which has also become a place for tourists to visit. It has been designed to allow people to look into the building, and the design challenges pre-conceived ideas of how car factories appear. Students read the text and answer questions 1–3.

> **Answers**
> 1 has hosted an opera, attracts tourists, includes a fine restaurant, and stands in the centre of the city among museums and churches
> 2 an interactive experience, a customer centre, and a restaurant
> 3 opera house, car plant, factory, museums, churches, and restaurant

2 If students don't know the meaning of the negative adjectives (e.g. *cramped*) encourage them to guess the meaning by looking in the text for opposite adjectives. If they still need help, you might need to explain the vocabulary, or you could encourage them to look the words up in a dictionary.

> **Answers**
> 1 well-equipped
> 2 state-of-the-art and / or up-to-date
> 3 spacious
> 4 beautifully maintained

3 42▷ You might need to play this listening twice.

> **Answers**
> 1 spacious, up-to-date
> 2 badly-equipped, run-down
> 3 old-fashioned

Watch out! Compound adjectives, such as *well equipped*, *badly equipped*, *well maintained*, *well located* etc., need a hyphen when they come before a noun, but not when they come after a noun. For example:
> *The office is **well equipped**.*
> *It's a **well-equipped** office.*

Extra activity

To focus on the intensifiers in **4**, play the listening again and ask students to number the intensifiers they hear according to which person uses them (speaker 1, 2, or 3).

Answers: *1 really 2 extremely, fairly 3 not exactly, pretty* (note also the use of *not very* in the listening).

4 Students complete the scale.

> **Answers**
> **1** not exactly   **3** really
> **2** fairly, quite, pretty   **4** extremely

Tip Refer students to the *Tip* and check understanding of the language point. Ask different students the following questions.

> *What's your job / course like?*
> *What was your weekend like?*

Students could also work in pairs and think of three similar questions to ask each other.

» If students need more practice, go to **Practice file 10** on page 120 of the **Student's Book**.

5 These sentences are from the listening, but students don't have to restrict themselves to the adverbs they heard. They can try putting different adverbs in the sentences to see how the meaning changes.

Watch out! Note that some adverb + adjective combinations are not possible because some adjectives are extreme adjectives. For example, you cannot use the adverbs *very* or *extremely* with the adjectives *amazing* or *state-of-the-art*.

6 42▷ Students listen and compare their sentences in **5** with the version in the listening. Answers that differ from the listening are not necessarily wrong.

> **Answers from the listening**
> **1** really   **5** not exactly
> **2** very   **6** very
> **3** fairly   **7** pretty
> **4** extremely

Pronunciation

You might like to draw students' attention to the fact that we stress the adverb in the sentence to add emphasis. Put the following sentences on the board and write the adverb in a different colour or underline it. Say a sentence and ask the class to repeat it. Once you have drilled them a few times, encourage students to use this pronunciation feature in the next exercise.

> *Your new offices are <u>really</u> amazing.*
> *It's all very <u>well</u> designed.*
> *Everyone is <u>extremely</u> friendly.*
> *All the machines are <u>fairly</u> old.*
> *It's <u>not exactly</u> state-of-the art.*
> *The offices are <u>not very</u> modern.*
> *They're a <u>pretty</u> successful company.*

7 Allow time for students to read the website. They can then describe the offices in pairs. You could then ask students to decide on the best offices for their company.

8 Students now make their own sentences about real places of work or leisure using adverb + adjective combinations.

Pre-work learners

Students can describe their place of study or where they live for the work-related places on the list.

Feedback focus

Focus on correct combinations of adverbs and adjectives. You could also monitor for word order and word stress.

ⓘ Refer students to the **Interactive Workbook Glossary** for further study.

Business communication skills

1 Discuss these questions as a class. Note that how suggestions are made may vary from company to company. Some businesses may have quite formal procedures for employee ideas. In other companies suggestions may arise during informal conversations (e.g. while chatting around the coffee machine).

Pre-work learners

Ask the students how they make suggestions or give feedback on their place of study and on their courses.

2 Students complete the comments with the phrases.

> **Answers**
> **1** why don't   **3** have you thought about
> **2** we could always   **4** Couldn't we do

Extra activity

Ask students what they think about the comments in **2**. Do they have a crèche or relaxation room where they work or study? What are they like?

3 43▷ Before listening, allow time for students to read about the situation.

4 The expressions here are all taken from the listening, so you can play it again to help or to check answers if necessary. This exercise draws students' attention to the different forms used in the language of suggesting and recommending. Some structures use the bare infinitive only and others the *-ing* form. If students need help with this exercise, they can refer to the *Key expressions*.

5 43▷ These expressions are used for responding positively or negatively to suggestions or recommendations.

Extra activity

For more practice of the expressions introduced in this section, students can work in pairs and take turns to say the sentences in **4** and choose a correct response from **5**. For example:
  A *I think we should consider having the crèche.*
  B *Good idea.*

≫ If students need more practice, go to **Practice file 10** on page 120 of the **Student's Book**. Students might need to refer to the *Key expressions*.

6 Students study the designs and lists of advantages and disadvantages. Discuss as a class whether they can identify any further advantages or disadvantages.

7 Students can prepare their recommendations alone or with another student who is looking at the same design.

When they are ready, put the students in A / B pairs for their discussion. Make sure they also use the expressions for responding. Refer them to the *Key expressions*.

8 Students work in groups of three or four. Tell students that this is a fairly informal meeting. They should begin by brainstorming, and any new ideas should be welcomed. Once they have generated a list of suggestions for their Anarchy Zone they should then reduce it to four items. During the presentation stage, encourage students to draw a sketch of the 'Zone' on the board if necessary. Also allow time for other groups to ask plenty of questions and make comments. A spirit of healthy competition for the best idea between groups will also help.

Feedback focus

After the discussion and presentations, give feedback on expressions used for suggesting and recommending. Students often find it particularly difficult to use the expressions for responding naturally, so you may also want to focus some comments on that.

ⓘ Refer students to the **Interactive Workbook Email** and **Phrasebank** sections for further study.

Practically speaking

1 Students could circle the linking words as well as underlining the reasons.

2 With weaker classes, students might want to write the sentences out in full, but if possible try to get students speaking and using the linkers introduced in **1**.

Language at work

1 Students work in pairs and make a list of facilities.

Possible answers
coffee lounge, fitness area, parking, showers, canteen, drinks machines, lockers, first aid

2 44▷ Students listen and write the facility.

Answers
1 c (lockers)
2 a (running machines / gym)
3 b (coffee lounge / relaxation area)

3 44▷ Ask students to read sentences 1–7 and guess the missing words before listening again.

Answers
1 much
2 any
3 a few
4 some
5 a lot of / a little
6 many
7 a few

4 At this level students should be familiar with the terms countable and uncountable nouns (or count / non-count). If not, provide the terms so that they can match them to the nouns in italics.

Answers
countable nouns: running machines, shelves, places, chairs, employees
uncountable nouns: spare time, space, clothes

Dictionary skills

To show students how to use their dictionaries to check if nouns are countable or uncountable, ask them to look up the words in **3**. Most dictionaries use the convention of the symbols [U] for uncountable and [C] for countable. Students will also find that good dictionaries will tell them which quantifiers precede countable nouns and which precede uncountable nouns.

5 Student should be able to categorize the quantifiers by studying the type of nouns that follow them in sentences 1–7 in **3**.

Answers
uncountable nouns: some, a lot of, any, much, a little
countable nouns: some, a lot of, any, many, a few

6 Students categorize the quantifiers.

Answers
1 a few, a little, some, not much, not many,
2 a lot, much, many
3 any, some, a lot, a few, a little
4 not much, not many, any, a lot

7 Students complete the sentences.

Answers
1 a lot of
2 any / some
3 a little
4 some / much
5 much

>> If students need more practice, go to **Practice file 10** on page 121 of the **Student's Book**.

8 Students look at the illustration in the *File*. Each sentence they make about the new layout should include a quantifier.

Possible answers
A lot of the employees are more relaxed.
There are a lot of chairs now.
There are some running machines.

Extra activity

For more practice of the quantifiers (especially *much* and *many*), students can role-play a situation between a host and a visitor. The host is showing the visitor around the new factory. The visitor has to ask questions about the factory and its facilities. For example:
How many people work here?
Do a lot of them use the fitness area?

9 To help start this exercise, brainstorm different facilities on the board. They can be facilities that students have at work or facilities they know other companies provide. Then give time for students to work alone and list facilities they have or would like to have before telling their partner.

Pre-work learners

Students talk about facilities for their place of study.

Feedback focus

As well as monitoring the class, you could also encourage students to monitor each other's use of quantifiers. Students should let each other know if they think there was an error.

(i) Refer students to the **Interactive Workbook Exercises** and **Tests** for revision.

Case study

Background

In this *Case study*, real examples of cause marketing are presented. This form of marketing involves collaboration between profit-making companies and charities. Students are encouraged to think about the possible results of such partnerships for those involved. They also discuss how companies might choose the charities they want to work with. The context for the *Task* is a similar collaboration between a company and a charity. Students then plan a charitable event, using language presented in the unit.

Find out if any of your students are already familiar with the term or concept of cause marketing. Students may work for larger firms which use this type of marketing. Allow time for students to read about cause marketing and the examples before moving on to the *Discussion*.

Discussion

1–3 Students can discuss the questions in pairs or small groups, before feeding back to the rest of the class.

> **Possible answers**
> 1 Both sides help to promote each other. The profit-making business sells more products and associates itself with a good cause so gains good publicity. The non-profit organization gains cheap advertising and raises money for its cause.
> 2 The companies probably chose these non-profit organizations because their typical customer base is also likely to be interested in these causes. For example, one of Yoplait's target markets will be middle-aged women, who will have a particular interest in the Foundation. Although there is no obvious link, students might also have some suggestions about why Vodafone chose to work with an autism charity. For example, as a mobile

> phone company, Vodafone emphasizes communication between individuals. Autistic people have problems connecting with others, so supporting such a charity ties in with the concept of improving communication.
> 3 One danger with this kind of partnership is if, for example, the profit business suffers some kind of PR disaster or gets bad publicity and this is then connected with the non-profit organization. Another problem could be if the business has to end its cause marketing to save money, because the charity may then suddenly lose a valued source of funds.

Task

1 Allow time for students to study the feedback and financial data from last year's open day in their *Files*.

2 Based on their information, students start the meeting by making recommendations. They then respond and discuss the best ideas for the next event. The meeting should last about fifteen minutes in total.

3 Students need time to prepare a presentation which can be given to the class. Encourage other students to ask questions. If you are short of time, students could take turns to present to another group and compare their ideas. Feedback should focus on how effectively students were able to present their recommendations.

One-to-one

Follow the *Case study* as given. For the *Task*, look at all the *Files* and discuss any recommendations together. Your student can then prepare and give a presentation.

>> Unit 10 Progress test and **Speaking test**, pages 104–105.

Unit content

By the end of this unit, students will be able to
- talk about the decision-making process
- participate in a discussion by giving opinions, agreeing, and disagreeing
- be persuasive
- use the first and second conditional for talking about future possibilities.

Context

The topic of *Decisions* and decision-making will be relevant to your students in their working lives and personal lives. In the business world, the difference in company culture and national culture can have a major affect on how decisions are made. Students may work in a company where decisions are made and strategies are developed at management level only, with the average worker rarely consulted. However, in companies or countries where a consensus approach is the norm, everyone in the company can be involved in the process. For example, in Japan unilateral consensus is very important, whereas in countries such as the USA or Britain, decision-making often occurs only at management level. However, due to the multi-national nature of businesses nowadays, such generalizations may no longer reflect reality. Different companies will have their own style of decision-making.

As part of their jobs, your students are likely to have to participate in meetings using English, and this can be especially difficult when native speakers are also involved. This unit provides students with phrases they will need for giving their opinions and contributing ideas to meetings in order to shape the final decision. It also presents language that can be used to persuade others, and this should help your students feel that they can have more of an influence on decision-making. Throughout the unit there are opportunities to use your students' experience of decision-making and meetings to inform class discussion on this topic. Note that if you are teaching a group from the same company, discussion of the decision-making process where they all work may need to be handled with care and sensitivity.

Starting point

1 Students work alone and read the four quotes. They can then discuss who they are most like with a partner.

Watch out! You might need to pre-teach the following:
instinct = a feeling that makes you do something or believe that something is true, even though it is not based on facts or reason.

2 Students can stay in their pairs or discuss this as a class. For many people, decisions at work are often made with much more planning than decisions at home. Students might be a different kind of decision-maker at work than they are at home.

Working with words

1 Students can read these texts alone and then discuss the differences as a class.

> **Possible answer**
> Suma involves everyone in the process from the beginning, whereas ideas at Mitsubishi seem to begin with management and then go to all the employees. With Ford the process is less democratic, with most decision-making taking place at management level only.

2 **45, 46, 47▷** Students match the listenings.

> **Answers**
> Audio 45: Ford
> Audio 46: Suma
> Audio 47: Mitsubishi

Extra listening

You could play the listening again and ask students to make notes on any advantages or disadvantages mentioned in the listening. Possible answers are as follows.

Audio 45: *One disadvantage is that managers might make decisions that the workers and union disagree with.*

Audio 46: *The advantages are that it generates lots of ideas and the speaker is happier about a decision if she's had some say.*

Audio 47: *One disadvantage is that decisions take a long time. The advantage is that they avoid confrontation and the problems which arise when you make up your mind too quickly.*

3 Discuss the question as a class (refer to the *Context*, which gives background information on these issues).

Pre-work learners

Ask students to consider the decision-making process in relation to
- family decisions at home
- decisions made in the students' school or college
- friends deciding where to go out for the evening.

4 **45**▷ Students listen and complete the words. They can then check their spelling by looking at the *Audio script*.

Answers
1 consultation   4 compromise
2 confrontation   5 consensus
3 concession(s)

Extra activity

Students work in pairs. Ask them to think of actual examples where they can use the five words in **4** in relation to their work. For example:

We often bring in experts for consultation on projects.

Pronunciation

Drill the word stress:

con<u>sen</u>sus, consul<u>ta</u>tion, confron<u>ta</u>tion, con<u>ces</u>sion, <u>com</u>promise.

---

5 **46**▷ With stronger students you could ask them to match the words and definitions before listening.

Answers
1 hierarchy   4 options   7 in favour of
2 brainstorm   5 backing   8 go for
3 put forward   6 majority   9 carry out

6 **47**▷ Students match the various verb + noun phrases before listening to compare their answers.

Possible phrases
put forward a suggestion / an opinion / an idea / ideas
have an opinion / a say / an idea / ideas
express an opinion
make major decisions / a suggestion
reach a consensus
evaluate ideas / an idea / a suggestion / an opinion
carry out major decisions / a suggestion
avoid confrontation
make up your mind

Dictionary skills

Good dictionaries contain examples of collocations (i.e. verb + noun phrases), so students may find it helpful to use them in conjunction with this exercise. Refer to the more specialized *Oxford Collocations Dictionary for Students of English* for full coverage of this vocabulary area. You might also like to encourage students to start recording common collocations alongside words in their notebooks.

Phrases in the listening
put forward an idea   evaluate (the) ideas
have a say   carry out (major) decisions
express (their) opinions   avoid confrontation
make suggestions   make up your mind
reach a consensus

⟫ If students need more practice, go to **Practice file 11** on page 122 of the **Student's Book**.

Tip Refer students to the *Tip*. They can make use of this language in the next exercise.

7 Students can try to use *so, now*, or *and* from the *Tip* to introduce their questions with the verb + noun phrases.

8 During this activity students don't necessarily have to use the vocabulary from this section, as this will happen in the reflective exercise that follows in **9**. Allow about five minutes at most for each discussion.

9 Before feeding back to the class, the groups can discuss and make notes on questions 1–3. When commenting on their discussion they should be using the verb + noun phrases from earlier.

Feedback focus

The group discussions in **8** should be fun, without too much concern for accuracy or use of certain language – it will be a useful review of functional expressions from previous units. Focus on the correct use and pronunciation of vocabulary from this section during exercise **9**.

ⓘ Refer students to the **Interactive Workbook Glossary** for further study.

Business communication skills

1 **48**▷ Before listening, ask students to read about the scenario. Draw a two-column table on the board. As a class discuss the reasons for choosing either of the two options and write some ideas in each column (see examples below).

shop in backstreets	*shop in centre outside of town*
good customer base	*may attract more customers*
in the centre	*higher profile / more upmarket*
easy to get to	*easy parking*

Allow time for students to read questions 1–7 before playing the listening.

Watch out! The listening refers to the centre being a *magnet for retailers*. Explain that a *magnet* attracts metal objects, so here the speaker uses it to emphasize how retailers will be attracted to the centre.

Answers
1 S (Stefan)
2 I (Ilse)
3 P (Patrick)
4 S (Stefan)
5 S (Stefan)
6 P (Patrick)
7 I (Ilse)

Extra activity

To help students listen for detail, write the following questions on the board. Students listen again and write the answers (shown in brackets).
1 *What is impossible in the current location? (parking)*
2 *Why can't they have two shops? (don't have financial resources)*
3 *Where did Ilse read about the centre? (in newspaper reports)*
4 *What can Jeff give? (expert advice)*
5 *What hasn't Jeff done? (played a computer game)*
6 *What has Jeff got? (years of experience)*

2 48▷ Students categorize the phrases. If students find this difficult, they could read the *Audio script*.

Answers
1 a, e
2 b, k, l
3 j
4 c, d, f
5 g, h,
6 i

Extra activity

For controlled practice of these phrases before the freer discussion in **4** students can work in pairs or threes. Refer them back to the discussion topic in the previous *Working with words* exercise **9** (1), in which they discussed the dress code for all staff. Explain that you want them to repeat the discussion, but this time they must try to use every phrase in **2**. As they use each phrase they tick it. The student who manages to use all the phrases first (and appropriately!) is the winner. By using the same topic, students can concentrate on the correct use of the phrases.

≫ If students need more practice, go to **Practice file 11** on page 122 of the **Student's Book**. Students might need to refer to the *Key expressions*.

3 Students work in pairs. Allow time for them to read the list of pros and cons. They then take turns to give opinions and respond to opinions.

4 Students can work in groups of three to five people. Allow time for students to study each discussion point first. Remind students to make use of the phrases in the *Key expressions*.

Feedback focus

Concentrate on the correct use of the phrases. At the end you could ask students to refer back to the questions in exercise **9** of the *Working with words* section and ask them to reflect on the discussion.

ⓘ Refer students to the **Interactive Workbook Email** and **Phrasebank** sections for further study.

Practically speaking

1 49▷ You might need to play this twice so that students can write the phrases down.

Answers
1 come on
2 let's face it
3 the thing is
4 to be honest

Watch out! Note that students need to be aware that the expression *come on* is rather direct and may be considered rude if used with someone you don't know very well.

2 Students match the phrases to the meanings.

Answers
a 3
b 1
c 4
d 2

3 Students discuss the statements. When giving feedback, focus on the use of the phrases in **1**, rather than on content.

Language at work

1 If you worked on the previous section of this unit, begin by eliciting the situation with the computer games shop (the owners need to decide whether to move to the shopping centre or stay where they are). Students then read the email and discuss the advice as a class.

Possible answer
Jeff will probably advise them not to move because they should be aiming to maintain their current customer base.

2 Students underline the correct verbs.

> **Answers**
> 1 had
> 2 don't keep
> 3 will

3 Students match the sentences and meanings.

> **Answers**
> 1 c
> 2 a
> 3 b

Watch out! At this stage you might want to spend some time working on the conditional forms, especially if students had problems choosing the correct verbs in the email. Students could begin by reading the language reference section in the *Practice file*. Check that students understand the following.

> The first conditional uses this verb structure: *If +* present simple, *will +* verb.
> The second conditional uses this verb structure: *If +* past simple, *could / would / might +* verb.

4 Before they match the words in *italics*, ask students which sentence is in the first conditional and which is in the second conditional (1 = first, 2 = second).

> **Answers**
> 1 if not = unless
> 2 just imagine = What if

>> If students need more practice, go to **Practice file 11** on page 123 of the **Student's Book**.

5 Students can either say or write answers to the questions.

Feedback focus

Monitor carefully and correct immediately if there are problems – don't wait until the end. Note that at this level students should be aware that they can contract *will / would* to *'ll / 'd* and should aim to do so when speaking. Raise the issue in feedback if they use the full form.

> **Answers**
> 1 win / 'll go   5 will you do / retire
> 2 listened to / would avoid   6 will you do / offer
> 3 'd understand / explained   7 would you react / relocated
> 4 cooperated / 'd make

6 Students can choose how likely / unlikely their responses are.

Pre-work learners

Write the following on the board:
> *What will / would you do if:*
> • *the course you want to do is / was in a college overseas?*
> • *your morning bus is / was cancelled and you have / had no public transport?*
> • *you get / got the qualification you want / wanted?*

Feedback focus

Focus on any difficulties students are having with the two conditional forms. Note that in many cases, the choice of the conditional will depend on the student's point of view.

Extra activity

For further practice, ask students to write an email. Write the following instructions on the board.
> *You are consultants and the computer shop has asked for your views on setting up an online business to sell their games. Your views are as follows.*
> • *low costs and overheads*
> • *existing customers use computer games and are comfortable using computers, so no problem with buying online*
> • *very competitive market now*
> • *difficult to attract new customers*

Students use these prompts to write an email. The email should contain a selection of first and second conditionals.

ⓘ Refer students to the **Interactive Workbook Exercises** and **Tests** for revision.

Activity

This *Activity* is fairly self explanatory, so allow students time to read the instructions and start the activity. Make sure that students are taking time to discuss each option carefully, before moving to the next box. This should generate a number of first and second conditionals.

Feedback focus

Part of your role during this activity may be helping with some of the vocabulary. However, you should also monitor for correct use of conditional forms and focus on any other key errors.

>> **Unit 11 Progress test** and **Speaking test**, pages 106-107.

12 Innovation

Unit content

By the end of this unit, students will be able to
- talk about innovation and describe new ideas
- give a formal presentation
- respond to questions and comments
- use the superlative form for talking about extremes and ranking ideas.

Context

The topic of *Innovation* is often associated with new inventions and inventors. However, while innovation is an important feature in the process of creating new devices or products, the term *innovation* can be applied more widely – it is the process of introducing something new, which could also mean a new way of doing something.

Modern business puts a great deal of emphasis on 'thinking outside the box' – or, in other words, trying to challenge accepted norms. By asking employees to look at something in a new way, companies hope to improve what they do. Often it is hoped that innovation will solve a perceived problem. This could be anything from a problem with the administration in a company, through to a problem with sales or the need to update a product or service.

While many companies are able to generate new ideas, fewer are able to successfully exploit or implement these ideas. An integral stage in the process is ensuring that everyone involved supports the new concept. If employees don't believe in or support the change, innovation will often fail. So for innovation to succeed, the people affected need answers to the following question: *What are the benefits of this change for me?*

This unit enables students to practise the vocabulary and expressions needed to present and discuss innovation. Students also have the opportunity to practise dealing with the type of difficult questions that often arise when people are confronted with change.

Starting point

Students work in pairs to order the objects. You can add a competitive element to this by giving points to each pair for every correct answer. They can then check their answers in *File 9* on page 137. Students can discuss the second question as a class.

Working with words

1 Briefly discuss this as a class.

2 Students read the text and answer the first question. You may wish to explain that the title *Food for thought* is an expression in English, meaning *lots to think about*, and doesn't usually refer to food. You could ask students why they think it is used here. For the second question, students will need to discuss why they would or wouldn't like to go. Encourage them to give reasons for their answer.

> **Answer**
> 1 To create an atmosphere where people are able to have their best new ideas.

Extra activity

Write the following words on the board: *three*, *badges*, *advice*, *innowaiters*, *happy*. Tell students that all these words are in the text. Ask students to write comprehension questions that would result in the words on the board as answers. Possible questions could be:
1 *How many courses are there in the meal?*
2 *What do customers wear?*
3 *What do customers give each other?*
4 *Who serves innovative ideas, as well as food and drink?*
5 *According to Ditkoff, how do people need to feel to get their best ideas?*

---

3 Students match the words to the definitions to check their understanding.

> **Answers**
> 1 concept
> 2 brainchild
> 3 innovative
> 4 'a-ha' moment
> 5 facilitators
> 6 catalyst
> 7 come up with (note change of tense from text)
> 8 obstacle
> 9 prototype

4 50▷ Before playing the listening, ask students to find the three questions in the text.

> **Answers**
> 1 How can I get a new job?
> 2 How can I find someone to invest in my prototype?
> 3 How can I start my own catering business?

5 50▷ Students listen for adjectives. You could ask students to predict the possibilities before listening.

Answers	Job / Company	Technology	Idea
dynamic	✓		
original			✓
reliable	✓		
revolutionary			✓
simple			✓
sophisticated		✓	
traditional	✓		

Note that there are other combinations. For example, *revolutionary technology* or *revolutionary company* are also acceptable. However, those in the listening are among the most common adjective + noun combinations.

Pronunciation

Drill the word stress in the following adjectives: *tra<u>di</u>tional, re<u>li</u>able, <u>dy</u>namic, revo<u>lu</u>tionary, so<u>phis</u>ticated, <u>sim</u>ple, o<u>ri</u>ginal*

▶▶ If students need more practice, go to **Practice file 12** on page 124 of the **Student's Book**.

6 Students discuss the questions in pairs.

Pre-work learners

Students work in pairs. Ask them to think of three companies they know well and describe what type of company they are. For example:

Microsoft is a revolutionary company.

Tip Refer students to the *Tip* about *invention* and *innovation*.

7 Allow about ten minutes for this discussion. Students can brainstorm ideas as if they are at the *Breakthrough café*. Afterwards they can report their best suggestions back to the class. To help with the next exercise, write some of the ideas in note-form on the board as each group presents. Alternatively, ask students to make notes on all the ideas they hear.

8 Refer students to the ideas on the board or their notes from **7**. Students then work alone and write their answers.

9 They now compare and discuss their answers in **8**.

10 For exercise 1, students simulate the situation at the *Breakthrough Café*. It will be helpful if you can give students badges to write on. You could use sticky labels like post-it notes, or address labels. Students write their *How can I...?* question on the label and stick it to their chest (note that it doesn't have to be work-related). Then ask everyone to stand up and walk around the room as if at a party. They should talk to each other and come up with suggestions. Allow five to ten minutes. Don't give any feedback on language in this activity. The aim is for students to generate ideas freely and develop their fluency.

For exercise 2, ask students to sit down after their 'party' and think about the different ideas they heard before asking them to report back to the class. Encourage students to use some of the adjectives in **5**.

Feedback focus

Focus on the correct use and pronunciation of the vocabulary presented in this section.

ⓘ Refer students to the **Interactive Workbook Glossary** for further study.

Business communication skills

1 Students study the mission statement and compare it with their companies' own mission statement.

Pre-work learners

Ask students if their college has a statement which tries to summarize its aims.

Alternative

If your students' company or college doesn't have a mission statement, ask them to try and write one in class.

Watch out! Many companies develop *mission statements* to help communicate their vision and direction not only to customers, but also throughout the company to all its employees. You can often find *mission statements* on company websites, although it's also surprising to discover how many employees have no idea what their company's *mission statement* is.

2 51▷ As a lead-in, ask students if they ever give or attend presentations in English. If so, ask students what they find difficult in these situations. Students then listen to the introduction of a presentation and correct the agenda.

Watch out! Note that in the listening students hear the speaker say: *I'm going to talk about where this company is.* You might need to explain that this does not refer to physical location, but is an expression commonly used to describe the current situation.

> **Answer**
> Points 1 and 2 are in the wrong order.
> 1 Current company situation
> 2 How we want to be seen
> 3 Finding a mission statement

3 **51**▷ Students order the phrases and then listen to check.

> **Answers**
> a 4   e 3
> b 7   f 6
> c 2   g 5
> d 1

4 **52**▷ Students listen and answer.

> **Answer**
> Words that describe the company, including the views of the oldest and newest customers.

5 **52**▷ Students listen again and complete the phrases for referring to visuals.

> **Answers**
> 1 let's look at this
> 2 As you can see,
> 3 You'll notice that

6 **53**▷ Students listen to Rudi's comment. They can then discuss whether they agree with him as a class.

> **Answer**
> He thinks that employees often have no idea what the mission statement of their own company is.

7 **53**▷ Students correct any mistakes and then listen to check.

> **Answers**
> 1 That's everything I want to say for the moment.
> 2 Thank you all for listening.
> 3 The main reason for this meeting is to …
> 4 Are there any questions?
> 5 We think it's a good idea because …

▶▶ If students need more practice, go to **Practice file 12** on page 124 of the **Student's Book**. Students might need to refer to the *Key expressions*.

8 By choosing something simple to present, students can focus on using expressions. Allow time for students to think of an object to present. Alternatively, you could assign an object to each student. If you think students will find this task difficult, they can work in pairs and prepare their one-minute presentations together.

Students look at the four stages of the presentation. Draw their attention to the suggested expressions for each stage. Make sure students realize that they can also use any of the other expressions in the *Key expressions*. Students will give full presentations in the next exercise, so you can focus on helping students with the expressions here, rather than on giving detailed feedback.

Watch out! If the students need more help, you might like to give a quick demonstration of what you want by picking up a pen and giving your own presentation. For example:
> *Today, I'm going to tell you about my pen. As you can see, it looks like an ordinary pen, but in fact it's the most important object in my life! The best thing about it is that I can mark your work, but it also does other things like allowing me to sign my name on cheques or draw pictures when I'm bored. Pens also affect the world. Presidents sign famous documents with pens …*

9 Students now reproduce the presentation in the listening, but for their own company. As part of the preparation you could hand out an overhead transparency with a pen, or a large piece of flipchart paper to each student. As they prepare they can design their visual aid with adjectives on. It might be helpful if students practise with a partner before presenting it to the whole class.

Alternative

To give students plenty of time to prepare and practise their presentations, you could set this as a homework task and have the presentations at the next lesson. Refer students to the *Phrasebank* section of the *Interactive Workbook* to help them revise the presentation phrases.

Pre-work learners

Students can create adjectives for an imaginary company or a famous company they know well or can easily research (via the Internet).

Feedback focus

If you have completed previous units in the book, students will now be used to giving mini-presentations in class. However, this is the first time they will have given a formal presentation. In addition to giving feedback on language, you might also wish to comment on the following areas:
- *structure* (was the presentation easy to follow?)
- *body language* (was it relaxed and not distracting?)
- *eye contact* (did they look at the audience?)

- *visual aids* (were they clear? did the student use them effectively or just read from them?)
- *delivery* (intonation that maintains interest? clear pronunciation?).

One way to approach this is to ask students what they think makes a good presentation and list their ideas on the board. You can then use this as the basis for your feedback. You could also encourage peer feedback, with students commenting on each other's work afterwards.

ⓘ Refer students to the **Interactive Workbook Email** and **Phrasebank** sections for further study.

Practically speaking

1 54▷ While students may feel confident preparing and giving a presentation, it becomes harder when they have to answer questions. Remind students that they can try to predict the kind of questions they might be asked and think of ways to answer them in advance. Begin by asking students how they usually handle difficult questions in presentations or in meetings. Then see if any of their ideas are listed in methods 1–6.

Play the listening to see what the presenter uses.

> **Answers**
> 3, 5, 4

2 Students match phrases a–f to methods 1–6.

> **Answers**
> a 1   d 5
> b 4   e 6
> c 2   f 3

3 Students take turns to ask and respond.

Extension

Each student writes three more questions to ask their partner. The partner needs to use an appropriate response.

Language at work

1 As a lead-in, ask students if they ever have meetings where the participants are not face-to-face. Elicit ideas such as *conference calling* and *video conferencing*. Ask students if they regularly use this kind of technology and what the advantages of it are (e.g. you don't have to travel long distances, you can communicate with anyone at any time).

Explain that this section of the unit will look at some of these ways of communicating. Your students should recognize superlative adjectives so this should act as a review and extension of the rules. Students read the text and correct the mistakes.

> **Answer**
> most valuable assets
> delivers the best sound quality
> that's the furthest of*
> participants are happiest
>
> * Note that a student may use the comparative *further than*, which is also acceptable here.

2 Students quickly answer the questions about DreamWorks.

Watch out! You might need to pre-teach the following: *high-grossing* = very profitable.

> **Answers**
> 1 films like Toy Story and Shrek 2
> 2 a new videoconferencing system

3 After students have underlined the form, ask them to work in pairs and compare answers.

> **Answers**
> For <u>most</u> people, DreamWorks Animation (DWA) is probably <u>best known</u> for producing films like *Toy Story* and, recently, *Shrek 2*, which was the <u>third highest</u>-grossing film of all time. However, the company's <u>latest</u> release isn't a film, but what may be the <u>most sophisticated</u> videoconferencing system the world has ever seen.

4 This clarifies the three main uses of the superlative.

> **Answers**
> 1 b
> 2 c
> 3 a

Watch out! Note that rule 2 may seem odd to students, as we often teach that the superlative is used to describe the maximum or minimum. However, we also often refer to the *second best* or *third best*.

》 If students need more practice, go to **Practice file 12** on page 125 of the **Student's Book**.

5 This exercise focuses on the third rule in **4**. Elicit one or two examples from the class in order to demonstrate the construction. Students then use the table to make questions. You could demonstrate by asking the following: *What's the worst decision you've ever made?*

6 You could lead into this by brainstorming types of new technology or recent innovations for communicating. For example: *email, mobile phones, video conference, webcams, conference calls, texting, online chat, and message boards.*

Pre-work learners

Ask them to think about how they communicate with family and friends.

Feedback focus

Give feedback on the superlative forms only.

---

i Refer students to the **Interactive Workbook Exercises** and **Tests** for revision.

Case study

Background

This *Case study* focuses on two modern innovations. Students are encouraged to think about how such innovations can be marketed and made profitable. In the *Task* students think of their own innovation and consider how they would market and promote their idea. They then give a presentation of their product, using language presented in the unit.

Allow students time to read the texts before moving on to the *Discussion*.

Discussion

1–3 Students discuss the questions in pairs or small groups before feeding back to the rest of the class. As an extension to question **2** ask students to think of two other potential users of these products. For example:

The Kenguru car might be popular with single drivers or commuters.
The pump may become popular to reduce electricity bills in general.

> **Possible answers**
> **1 Kenguru car:** small, stylish and easy to park, gives user freedom and independence.
> **Pump:** powered by sun's heat, needs no electricity, has no moving parts, cheap to produce.
> **2 Kenguru car:** wheelchair users.
> **Pump:** farmers or manufacturers of central-heating.

> **3 Kenguru car:** could be targeted at wheelchair users, health-care centres, and hospitals. It might also be targeted at old people's homes.
> **Pump:** could be marketed to governments and NGOs in countries in the developing world. With global warming and scarce water resources, the market demand may also grow around the world.

Task

1 Allow no more than ten minutes for students to think of different things that need improving in their everyday lives. These could be as varied as the time needed to clean the house, to the shortage of cycle paths. After ten minutes, ask the groups to choose one of the problems and think of ways to solve it. If possible, provide large sheets of paper so that students can draw their ideas.

If you think that your students might find it difficult to think of ideas, you could write the following example on the board: *How could we improve transport in the local community?* You could then ask students to brainstorm ideas in the following two categories (possible answers in brackets).

Changes	*Products*
(introduce congestion charges)	*(flat escalators on main routes)*
(build more cycle lanes)	*(motorized skateboards)*
(reduce cost of public transport)	*(rickshaws)*

2 Students will need to show designs and visual aids relating to their brainchild, so allow time for them to prepare these. Note that these are group presentations, so students need to decide who will deal with each stage of the presentation. They should practise the presentation at least once. Remind them to think about the questions they may be asked at the end and how they will answer them. Feedback should focus on the quality of the presentations and correct use of the language introduced in this unit.

Alternative

Divide the class into two groups. Explain that they need to attract investment for a new invention. They will have to prepare and give a presentation to a group of investors. Assign one group the Kenguru car and the other group the pump. In their presentations they can use ideas discussed during the *Case study* by describing how the product works, its selling points, and the target customers.

One-to-one

Let your student choose one of the inventions from the *Background* to present.

» **Unit 12 Progress test** and **Speaking test**, pages 108–109.

Unit content

By the end of this unit, students will be able to
- talk about breakdowns and faults
- discuss problems and difficulties
- offer advice
- check someone understands what was said
- use the language of advice and recommendation for offering help
- use *too* and *enough* for describing problems.

Context

The topic of *Breakdown* and faulty items is one that all students can relate to, whether they are looking at it from the perspective of the customer or of the supplier. Most students will have unknowingly bought or supplied something with defects. Technical defects can be particularly difficult to deal with because they require expertise to resolve them.

Anticipating faults has almost become an accepted practice in modern business. Companies need to assess the balance between the cost of producing high-quality products and the price that the modern consumer is prepared to pay. Companies may decide to cope with a higher number of returns or faults in order to charge less and sell more. In such circumstances, standards of customer service can be affected and you might like to refer students back to *Unit 5*, which dealt with the issue of what makes good customer service. The topic also goes beyond technical faults and into the area of communication breakdown between staff.

The unit provides students with language that would enable them to describe problems and discuss solutions. Your students are likely to find themselves in a position at work where they need to contact someone about a problem, or where they need to react to someone else's problem. Students have the opportunity to practise dealing with these situations throughout the unit and this should enable them to feel confident when dealing with such issues.

Starting point

Students can discuss these questions as a class. Examples of breakdowns might include: *engines in cars, machinery, electrical goods, central heating, air conditioning*. Note that we can also talk about a breakdown in communications or in the systems at work. With the second question, an immediate response might be that breakdowns are never acceptable, but the reality is that they are inevitable and the cost of accepting breakdowns may mean that the price for the customer can be kept down.

Extension

Elicit examples of when students have bought items from shops or suppliers which have failed to work or have had a fault. Ask the following questions:
- How did you feel about it?
- What did you do?
- Should customers accept imperfect products as the norm?

Working with words

1 As a lead-in you could ask any students who supply goods or services to describe their company's policy on defects. Then ask them to look at the three examples in **1** to see if they are similar.

Watch out! You might need to pre-teach the following:
refund = money that is paid back to you because you returned a product to a shop.

Allow time for students to match the statements to the products. Ask them to underline the words which helped them choose their answers.

Answers
1 c (electrical products)
2 a (food products)
3 b (clothing)

2 The words in **bold** all refer to faults, so by matching the definitions, students should see the subtle differences.

Answers

1	defective	3	defect
2	damaged	4	failure

Pronunciation

Draw attention to the change in word stress with *defect* and *defective*.

3 Students match the sentence halves. They can then check their answers in pairs.

Answers	
1 c	5 a
2 g	6 f
3 e	7 d
4 h	8 b

Dictionary skills

Although the words in **3** are all linked by the same topic, students should be encouraged to record what part of speech they are (verb, adjective, noun). It will be helpful for them to use dictionaries to check the meaning and the part of speech. They may also want to note any related word forms that they find in the dictionary. For example, students can record the adjective, the negative prefix, and the noun form as follows:

reliable – unreliable – reliability
compatible – incompatible – compatibility
understanding – misunderstanding – understandable.

4 Students categorize the words in **1** and **3**. Note that some of the words do not fit into the categories because they are very specific. For example, the adjective *down* in this case usually refers to phone lines, power cables, or the Internet. A *bug* is also specific to computers or other objects with micro-chip technology inside.

Possible answers
1 let us down, unreliable, misunderstanding
2 defective, defect, damaged, faulty, incompatible, failure
3 let us down, unreliable

>> If students need more practice, go to **Practice file 13** on page 126 of the **Student's Book**.

5 You could add a competitive element to this by finding out which pair managed to use the most number of words (appropriately) for each picture. Students can tick the words in **1** and **3** as they use them.

Possible answers
a gone wrong, faulty, out of order, unreliable
b defective, defect, down, unreliable, bug, faulty, incompatible
c down, gone wrong, (power) failure, faulty
d misunderstanding, unreliable

6 Before students begin this activity, draw their attention to the fact that the example sentence uses an *if*-clause (a zero conditional), and they can use the same structure to discuss the problems.

Extra activity

Ask students to choose five of the new words and use them to write their own sentences about their work.

Feedback focus

Focus on the correct pronunciation and appropriate use of vocabulary presented in this section.

ⓘ Refer students to the **Interactive Workbook Glossary** for further study.

Business communication skills

1 Discuss these two questions as a class. Then ask students who is in charge of fixing things at work. For example, is there an IT department that deals with computer problems?

Pre-work learners

Students can say whether they often fix things at home, such as their bicycle, computer, or electrical equipment.

2 55▷ Ask students to only write words or short notes in the table while listening.

Watch out! You might need to pre-teach the following: *diagnosis* = what someone thinks is the reason for the problem, e.g. a doctor makes a diagnosis for a patient.

Answers
1 **Situation / problem:** in an office – boss gives too much work
Diagnosis: poor communication
Solution / cure: speak to her and explain how you feel, ask for an extension on deadline
2 **Situation / problem:** in a shop – faulty laptop; it crashes
Diagnosis: battery problem
Solution / cure: buy a new battery

3 55▷ You might need to play the listening twice to give students time to complete the phrases. They can check their answers or find any missing words afterwards, by turning to the *Audio script*.

Answers

1	matter	9	How
2	keeps	10	exactly
3	mean	11	always
4	like	12	say / mean
5	tried	13	sounds
6	were	14	best
7	think	15	should
8	sort		

Watch out! Note the construction *If I were you …* in question 6. Students might ask why it isn't *If I was …*, so explain that either is possible, although we tend to use the more traditional *were* when giving advice.

4 Students categorize the phrases in **3**.

Answers

a	1, 9	d	4, 13
b	2, 11	e	5, 6, 7, 14
c	3, 10, 12	f	8, 15

5 Students work alone and re-order the conversation before comparing with a partner and practising the conversation.

Answers

2	h	5	b	8	j
3	f	6	a	9	c
4	e	7	d	10	i

Tip This *Tip* is worth paying particular attention to. Students were advised to use the present simple with adverbs of frequency in *Unit 1*, but can now see this rule being broken. Explain that this adverb of frequency + present continuous form is a special construction used for describing annoying habits. To give students further practice, ask them to write down three annoying habits of people they know and then tell their partner.

Extra activity

For more practice of the phrases in **3**, students can work in pairs and recreate the two dialogues in the listening.

» If students need more practice, go to **Practice file 13** on page 126 of the **Student's Book**. Students might need to refer to the *Key expressions*.

6 Refer students to the *Key expressions* to help them prepare for these conversations. Students can then work in pairs and take turns to be A or B.

7 Students work in groups and take turns to speak for a minute on one of the subjects. The rest of the group can time them. The group conversations that follow will be fairly similar to those in **6**, although students don't need to follow the flow chart format so rigidly.

Pre-work learners

Students can have similar discussions about consumer goods used in their homes, or unreliable friends / people at college.

Extra activity

Ask each student to write down one problem they have (real or imaginary), and then tell their group about it. The rest of the group can then try to offer various solutions.

Feedback focus

Focus on the correct use of the expressions. Pay particular attention to correct use of the *-ing* form that follows many of these expressions. For example:
> It keeps on break*ing* down.
> Have you tried talk*ing* to her?

i Refer students to the **Interactive Workbook Email** and **Phrasebank** sections for further study.

Practically speaking

Extra activity

Before listening for language, you could ask the students to listen to the four situations and decide what the problem is, or what is being explained.
> Answers: **1** *communication at work*, **2** *how to complete an incident form*, **3** *the computer has crashed*, **4** *how to deal with a problem at work by speaking to the manager.*

1 **56▷** As a lead-in, ask students if people sometimes don't understand them. If so, ask what they can say to check the listener understands. Write their ideas on the board so that they can be compared with the expressions in the next exercise. Students then listen and match the two halves.

Answers

1	d	3	b
2	a	4	c

2 **56▷** Students listen again.

Answers

The listener in 2 and 3 doesn't understand.

3 If necessary you could play the listening again, so that students hear the words in 1–4 in context before answering.

> **Answers**
> **person understands**: 1 and 4
> **person doesn't understand**: 2 and 3

4 Allow time for students to make notes to help them prepare their explanations. Students then take turns to explain and check understanding, using the expressions in **1**.

Pre-work learners

Alternatives for discussion could be
- how to revise for an exam
- how to choose a good English course
- how to avoid doing too much work in class.

Language at work

1 As a lead-in, ask students the following questions: *Who do you often give advice to? Who do you take advice from? What was the last piece of good (or bad) advice you gave or received?*

After discussing these questions, students categorize the sentences.

> **Answers**
> 1 e, f   3 d
> 2 a, c, g   4 b

2 This introduces students to the use of *too* and *enough* with adjectives and nouns. This language will be particularly useful for explaining problems.

> **Answers**
> 1 Is the job too <u>difficult</u>?
> 2 I don't have enough (time.)
> 3 It's <u>easy</u> enough to do.

3 Students should focus on the sentences in **2** to help them answer this question.

> **Answer**
> both

4 Students now focus on the use of *too*.

> **Answer**
> It's used to say that something is more than ideal.

5 Students choose the correct answers.

> **Answers**
> 1 adjectives
> 2 before / after

» If students need more practice, go to **Practice file 13** on page 127 of the **Student's Book**.

Tip Ask students to read the *Tip* and then prepare one piece of advice and one prediction of their own using *should*. They then work in pairs and say their sentence to their partner. The partner can say how useful the advice is and if they agree with the prediction.

6 Students turn to their *Files*. Point out that the student who is explaining the problem could use *too* and *enough*. For example: *I'm wasting too much time going to see them, it isn't cool enough.*

The student giving advice can refer to the *Key expressions* list in the *Business communication skills* section.

7 Students should first discuss and identify the problems. They then role-play the situation.

> **Possible answers**
> a Someone badly dressed at a job interview.
>   A You should always wear a good quality suit for an interview.
>   B I don't have enough money to buy one.
> b Someone has too much work to do.
>   A You could ask a colleague to help you.
>   B No, it would take too long to explain how to do the work.
> c Someone is asleep at work.
>   A If I were you, I'd go to bed earlier
>   B I don't feel tired enough to sleep until 1.00 a.m.
> d Someone is stuck in a traffic jam on the way to work.
>   A You have to call your boss.
>   B I haven't got enough credit on my mobile phone.

Feedback focus

Students should find it fairly straightforward to use the phrases a–g in **1**, but may need more help when using *too* and *enough*.

ⓘ Refer students to the **Interactive Workbook Exercises** and **Tests** for revision.

Case study

Background

This *Case study* looks at the theme of ethics in business and balancing the needs of the suppliers, employees, and customers. It also highlights how the World Wide Web has changed the nature of business by making many different markets more accessible.

After students have read about One World Bazaar ask the class if they know of any similar organizations operating in this way.

Discussion

1–2 Students can discuss these questions in pairs before feeding back to the rest of the class.

> **Possible answers**
>
> 1 The producers benefit from this arrangement.
>   This could be seen as a good thing for the producers because it gives them a fair price, guarantees them an income, and allows them to produce what they like using available materials. The company also benefits as the producers are likely to be more loyal. However, it could also be seen as bad because it might lead producers to become complacent and produce lower standards of work.
>
> 2 Problems with this arrangement could be that it ignores customer needs. It may also result in poorer quality products for the customer, and they might well be able to find better quality products at lower prices elsewhere.

Task

1 Students read the details about problems at One World Bazaar. Ask the class what sort of complaints they think the company may be receiving in the three categories. Elicit examples for each category, for example:
   problems with using the website for online ordering – not secure, crashes
   poor quality / condition of goods received – often faulty
   problems with supply and delivery times – poor packaging, late.
Students work in groups of three. They each take a role and turn to their *File*. They will need about five minutes to read the information they have and prepare summaries for their colleagues.

2 When the students are ready, they can present their summaries.

3–5 Students listen to the summaries and then discuss ways to improve the situation for customers. When giving feedback, discuss the outcomes of the *Task* and ask students to think about what language they found useful or what they found difficult to talk about. You may be able to provide some useful expressions to help them with this kind of task in the future.

One-to-one

The student can turn to Student A's *File* and then discuss the complaints with you and suggest solutions. Then repeat the same process with the information for Student B and C if you have time.

» Unit 13 Progress test and Speaking test, pages 110–111.

14 Processes

Unit content

By the end of this unit, students will be able to

- talk about technical and non-technical processes
- make and change appointments or future plans
- use formal and informal expressions in emails
- get someone's attention and interrupt appropriately
- use the passive for talking about a process.

Context

The topic of *Processes* is often connected with mechanical systems or how something is manufactured, and there is no doubt that students involved in industry or production will be well aware of how important it is to be able to describe such processes. However, non-technical processes, such as how something is administered (e.g. an order or a job application), will also be relevant to most students. They will need to know how to present processes and procedures clearly. They will also need to understand explanations of processes and feel able to ask for clarification. This unit presents the language that students will need in order to communicate effectively in these situations. It also enables students to practise the passive voice, since this is important when describing processes.

This unit also provides the language for inviting and planning future contact. This is a crucial part of the socializing and networking process. The issue of appropriate register when socializing or writing emails is also addressed. It can often be difficult to know what level of formality is suitable in different situations. Students are encouraged to think about this issue and make decisions about the language they use in various contexts.

Starting point

Students brainstorm stages. They can then compare stages and note parts of the process which could be cut. You could collate everyone's ideas and draw a flow chart of the processes on the board.

> **Possible answers**
> **applying for a job**
> see job advert ➔ write letter and CV ➔ attend interview
>
> **moving your office**
> find new location ➔ book removal firm ➔ send out new contact details ➔ decide what needs to be moved where
>
> **buying a house**
> decide budget ➔ compare estate agents ➔ choose one ➔ look at houses ➔ apply for mortgage ➔ make an offer ➔ move in

Working with words

1 Discuss the first question as a class. Students then read the text and answer the other questions.

> **Answers**
> 1 Biodiesel is different to petrol-based fuel because it is made out of plants and vegetable oils.
> 2 No, it has been used for centuries.

Ask students if they know of any companies similar to D1 Oils in their own countries. Note that in certain countries biofuels are already used in cars on a regular basis.

2 57▷ Students listen to the end of the presentation and answer questions 1–3.

> **Answers**
> 1 The procedure is fairly simple.
> 2 There are two main stages: growing and processing.
> 3 The end product is a good quality fuel which you can use in any transport vehicle.

3 57▷ Before listening, allow time for students to study the pictures. Check that everyone understands the vocabulary. In this exercise students are listening for verb phrases. They do not necessarily write them exactly as they are said in the listening.

> **Answers**
> 1 Make / out of   4 taken out
> 2 pick up   5 Mix / heat
> 3 Feed / into   6 Put / into

Watch out! All the verb phrases in **3** are transitive – they must be followed by an object (*take out the oil*) and the object can separate the verb from the particle in each case (*take the oil out*).

Tip Note that the use of *pick up* in *Unit 6* referred to collecting someone by car from somewhere (e.g. an airport).

Language at work

1 Discuss the questions as a class. Check that students understand the term *networking*, which refers to meeting and talking to other people (socially) who may be useful or helpful to you in your work. With experienced students, build up a list of tips from them on how to network successfully. They will be able to compare this with the guidelines that follow in **2**.

2 60▷ Students read the eight points for effective networking before listening and ticking the points the speaker refers to. Make sure students realize that all eight points are important – not just the ones mentioned.

> **Answers**
> - Do your research before the event. ✓
> - Make sure you meet new people.
> - Start conversations by mentioning someone you both know. ✓
> - Pay attention to the speaker.
> - Introduce other people to each other.
> - Find someone to introduce you to the person you want to meet. ✓
> - Learn people's names and don't forget them.
> - Don't leave without the numbers of important contacts.

3 61▷ Explain to students that the verbs in sentences 1–5 are all in the passive form. Students complete the sentences and then listen and check.

Watch out! At this level students should have already been introduced to the present simple in the passive form. If not, or if you think they need more help with this, you could do the following *Extra activity* before moving on.

Extra activity

Write sentence 1 on the board in its passive and active form as follows.

> *Business is done through networking and meeting people.*
> *People do business through networking and meeting people.*

Then ask students the following questions.
- What is the tense in both sentences? (present simple)
- Why are we more likely to say the first sentence? (because we are interested in '*Business*' rather than '*People*')
- How is the passive formed? (*to be* + past participle)

The sentences include passive verbs in different forms. However, the exercise only requires students to write the past participle, and raises their awareness of the forms. If your students need more help at this stage, ask them to read the language reference in *Practice file 14* on page 129 of the *Student's Book* first. You might also like to refer students to *Irregular verb list* on page 134 of the *Student's Book*, for help with past participles.

> **Answers**
> 1 done   4 given
> 2 won / lost   5 introduced
> 3 invited

4 This draws attention to the form of the passive with other tenses and verb structures.

> **Answers**
> a 5   d 2
> b 3   e 1
> c 4

5 Students now consider the reasons for using the passive.

> **Answers**
> 1 a (it may also be 2, although it is likely that the mutual contact person's name will be mentioned in the conversation that follows), d
> 2 b, c
> 3 b, c

>> If students need more practice, go to **Practice file 14** on page 129 of the **Student's Book**.

6 All five statements are in the passive form. Students decide if they are true for them and if not, change them to make them true. They then tell their partner.

Pre-work learners

Your students could comment on the following statements.
- My college / university was founded over 100 years ago.
- Grades are lowered for late assignments.
- Students at my college are expected to complete their studies in under four years.
- In my country, education is paid for by the government.
- Essays in my college have to written in English.

Extra activity

Ask students to write five more sentences about their work (or studies). They must try to use all five structures from **4**. They then compare their sentences with a partner.

7 Students might want to base their presentations on the example in the listening. They could look at the *Audio script* for ideas. They don't have to use the passive throughout, but they should use it wherever appropriate.

Pre-work learners

Students can give presentations on
- how to write the perfect essay
- disciplinary procedures at college
- how to survive on a student loan.

Feedback focus

Make notes on the correct and incorrect use of the passive in the presentations, both in terms of form and use. For example, students might say the form correctly, but use a passive where an active form would sound more natural.

ⓘ Refer students to the **Interactive Workbook Exercises** and **Tests** for revision.

Case study

Background

This *Case study* looks at procedures and processes at airports. Students read about an airline that is trying to find technical solutions to delays at check-in. Students discuss possible solutions and their impact on customer satisfaction and airport security. This situation is the context for the *Task*, and students have the opportunity to practise the language from the unit when they present various check-in processes.

Allow time for students to read about Air27. You could ask them to underline the problems facing the airline and the causes. (Problems: no investment in technology for checking-in, passengers wait 2 hours, not enough staff in busy times, long queues, unhappy passengers, stress for staff, delayed flights or taking off without passengers, increased security measures.)

Discussion

1–3 Students can discuss these questions as a class or in pairs. If students are unfamiliar with air travel, you may need to help them. Answers to question 1 will vary.

> **Possible answers**
> **2** Other methods include
> - tickets with barcodes that can be scanned into machines at the airport
> - a code number you type into a self check-in machine
> - an online checking-in link on the company's website.

3

	Advantages	Disadvantages
1 for passengers	• faster / less time waiting • fewer queues • online booking and checking-in allows more flexibility in ticket choice / seat	• impersonal • passengers may make mistakes entering information • assumes everyone uses computers, or is comfortable with technology • real check-in staff ask security questions, unlike machines, so airline security may be compromised • luggage still has to be checked in as normal
2 for airlines	• cheaper in long term (once investment is made) • fewer staff required • easier to fill planes	• needs large initial investment in technology • passengers will need help using the technology

Task

1 Students will need time to study their *Files* and prepare their mini-presentations.

2 Students should be using the passive form while explaining the new systems.

3 During this discussion, students could refer to the list of advantages and disadvantages they made in the *Discussion* section to help them. At the end, each group can present their final decision and give their reasons. Encourage groups to give feedback on each other's solutions. You can also give feedback on their presentations of the new systems.

One-to-one

Look at each *File* with your student and discuss each of the new systems. Ask the student to choose the best solution. Alternatively, work as a pair with Student A and B's *Files* only.

» **Unit 14 Progress test** and **Speaking test**, pages 112–113.

Unit content

By the end of this unit, students will be able to
- talk about personal qualities
- appraise performance and set objectives
- tell a story
- use the past continuous and past perfect for talking about past events.

Context

The topic of *Performance* is relevant to everyone. The criteria by which we all define successful performance may vary quite widely. Traditionally and stereotypically, performance in business has been measured in terms of how much money is made or the position an individual may rise to within a company. However, there is now a greater emphasis on a good work-life balance. This means that some people may define success in terms of their quality of life and how far they are able to balance their work and their home-life.

Another concept that arises in this unit is motivation. This is a key issue when managing staff. Implementing ways of motivating and encouraging staff is something many companies spend time considering. Incentives such as bonus schemes or awards like 'employee of the month' can help. Performance reviews, where an employee and his / her line manager talk about past achievements and formulate new objectives, also help companies to motivate and manage staff effectively. This unit provides students with language that will help them to encourage and appraise staff effectively. Students have the opportunity to role-play an appraisal so that they can practise expressions needed when reviewing performance.

Starting point

Students can discuss these questions in pairs. Allow a few minutes for students to read the list in question 2 and tick the important factors. Encourage them to add any more they can think of. Students can then compare what they have ticked and explain their reasons, before feeding back to the rest of the class.

Working with words

1 As a lead-in, ask students how important it is for individual success to be recognized at work or school. They can then quickly scan the article for the answers.

> **Answers**
> 1 He isn't surprised because his staff are so enthusiastic and motivated.
> 2 members of staff or patients

Tip Note the distinction between the adjective and noun form of *patient*, both of which appear in the text and may cause confusion.

2 Discuss these questions as a class. As part of the discussion suggest or elicit some of the other ways success can be recognized, e.g. *a bonus scheme, an extra day off, a prize or award, promotion, a certificate.* Note that some people might think that this kind of award divides staff and creates bad feeling.

Pre-work learners

Ask students if they have something similar at their college, like 'student of the month'.

3 The description of each person matches to the adjectives in the earlier text.

> **Answers**
> 1 flexible
> 2 hard-working, motivated, dedicated
> 3 helpful, motivated (caring would also be possible)
> 4 caring, patient
> 5 enthusiastic
> 6 dependable

4 Students work in pairs and tell each other about a person they would nominate. Make sure they are using some of the adjectives.

Pre-work learners

Students can discuss people that might be nominated for 'student of the month'.

5 Students build nouns from the adjectives.

Dictionary skills

This is a good opportunity for students to make use of dictionaries, either to help them find the noun form, or to check their answers at the end of the task.

Answers
1 patience, confidence
2 dedication, motivation, ambition
3 enthusiasm
4 punctuality, flexibility, creativity, dependability

Extra activity

Ask students to decide what prefix is needed to make each adjective negative. For example:

impatient, unpunctual, inflexible, uncreative, unmotivated, undependable, unenthusiastic, unambitious, and *unconfident.*
Note that *dedicated* does not take a prefix.

Read the adjectives and nouns aloud and ask students to mark the word stress. Remind students that the word stress of the adjectives doesn't change with the negative prefix. Again, students could refer to their dictionaries to check.

Suggest to students that they record this new vocabulary in their notebooks as shown below. They could also add the translation and an example sentence.

Adjective	**Noun**	**Negative adjective**
patient	*patience*	*impatient*
dedicated	*dedication*	

6 Students complete the sentences and say if they are true or false. They can then discuss their answers with a partner.

Answers
1 flexibility	4 confidence
2 patient	5 motivation / dedication
3 punctuality	6 dedicated

➤➤ If students need more practice, go to **Practice file 15** on page 130 of the **Student's Book**.

7 Students think of three job titles and decide on two of the qualities (the nouns in **5**) that would be useful for the job.

Alternative

Write the following jobs on the board:
- *freelance designer*
- *sales representative*
- *customer care assistant*
- *computer programmer.*

Students work in pairs and discuss each noun in **5**. They must decide if the quality is necessary, useful, or not important for the job in question. For example:

Creativity is important if you want to be a freelance designer, but punctuality is not so important if you work from home.

8 Students can talk about their own job and describe the qualities they need.

Alternative

Put students in pairs. One student thinks of a job. The other has to guess the job, but can only ask *Yes/No* questions. They should ask about qualities needed. For example:
A *Do you need to be very ambitious for this job?*
B *Yes.*
A *And is it important to be a very confident person?*
B *Yes.*
A *Is it the Managing Director?*
B *Yes.*

You could write the names of jobs on cards for students to use if you like, e.g. *lawyer, football player, police officer, pilot, chef, journalist, stockbroker, management consultant.*

ⓘ Refer students to the **Interactive Workbook Glossary** for further study.

Business communication skills

1 Ask students to read the performance review and discuss whether they have something similar at work. If so, ask how often performance reviews occur and if they find such forms useful.

Watch out! Note that in many companies, an employee may have a performance review once or twice a year. This involves discussing their progress at work and setting personal aims and objectives. The first part of such a process often begins with an employee filling in a form. This is then given to the manager before the performance review meeting and forms the basis for the discussion.

Pre-work learners

Discuss what students think the purpose of such a form is and if they ever complete a similar form before meeting tutors at their college.

2 62▷ Answers can be in note-form. The main aim is that they can report back to their partner afterwards.

3 62▷ Students could try to match the two halves before listening again to check their answers.

Tip Refer students to the *Tip*. You can mention other examples of how we use past tenses to sound less direct. For example:

Something I thought you might like to do is …
I was wondering if you would like to join us.

4 63▷ Students listen to the rest of the meeting and answer the questions. Note that they need to write down phrases for question 1 and 3.

>> If students need more practice, go to **Practice file 15** on page 130 of the **Student's Book**. Students might need to refer to the *Key expressions*.

5 Students complete the appraisal form. If necessary, students can create an imaginary job.

6 Before this activity, you could review the phrases needed for the four stages with the class, or refer them to the *Key expressions*. If you have students from different levels of the company in the class, you will need to be sensitive when putting pairs together.

Feedback focus

Focus on the correct use of the phrases. You could also comment on how encouraging and motivating the managers were.

7 Students discuss any of the three areas and decide on a plan of action.

ⓘ Refer students to the **Interactive Workbook Email** and **Phrasebank** sections for further study.

Practically speaking

1 64, 65▷ Play the two versions and discuss the differences as a class.

2 64▷ Play the first listening only.

3 Don't let students spend too long thinking of jobs they have recently finished. They can be simple things, e.g. *fixed the computer, painted the house, made coffee for everyone*.

Language at work

1 Students read the extract and mark the statements.

2 Students focus on the tenses to match the sentences to the uses.

3 Once students have matched the tenses to the sentences ask students to say what the forms are: *had / have* + past participle, *was / were* + present participle.

>> If students need more practice, go to **Practice file 15** on page 131 of the **Student's Book**.

Unit conten

By the end of this

- talk about th
  achievement:
- report back c
- generalize
- use contrasti
  positive poin

Context

Typically, busines
terms, such as sa
turnover. Howeve
what you do is nc
success. Compar
factors contribut(
be, for example,
the environment,
healthy work-life

As well as seekir
companies are fa
maintain 'numbe
business environ
the other hand, s
mean helping a
a service, giving
learning somethi

Setting tasks wi
companies to m
these tasks and
that many empl
this reporting wi
coming to a con
this unit studen
and talking abou
have arisen whe
unit they will als
success and ac
or their own car

4 66▷ Students listen to two stories about performance reviews and make notes.

> **Answers**
>
> **Helena**
> 1 The Production Manager said she had to work as part of a team.
> 2 Because she'd said it was difficult being the only woman and he said she'd never get anywhere in the company.
> 3 Six months later she was transferred, and another six months after that was running the factory.
>
> **Matthias**
> 1 The HR Manager said he was doing well.
> 2 During the interview the HR Manager answered the phone and replied to an email. Then he was handed a review to sign which he wasn't given time to read. The written review was also different from what he had been told.
> 3 Matthias left the company and the HR Manager got fired.

5 66▷ Students complete the sentences before listening.

> **Answers**
>
> | | |
> |---|---|
> | 1 was working | 4 were talking |
> | 2 had already discussed | 5 had prepared |
> | 3 was running | 6 'd already left |

Watch out! Sentences 2 and 6 in **5** illustrate how we often use the word *already* in conjunction with the past perfect. Point this out to students and also remind them that *'d* is the contracted form of *had*.

6 Students create their own sentences about the timeline using the past perfect and past continuous. Note that they are also allowed to use the past simple, which they will need to show contrast. Students might need to write their sentences down initially.

> **Possible answers**
>
> She had a bad performance appraisal while she was working for the food company.
> She transferred to another subsidiary after she had had a bad performance appraisal.
> She was working in a subsidiary when she was asked to run it.
> She was asked to run the subsidiary after she had been transferred.

7 Students create a similar timeline for themselves, before describing it to their partner.

Alternative

Students can draw their timeline and describe it to their partner. The partner cannot see the timeline and must try to draw it so that it looks like the original.

ⓘ Refer students to the **Interactive Workbook Exercises** and **Tests** for revision.

Case study

Background

This *Case study* deals with presentation skills and the training requirements for employees who will need to present in English (something that many international business people are now expected to be able to do). Students are encouraged to discuss how to give a good presentation and this provides the context for the *Task*, where students are able to practise appraising performance using language from the unit.

67▷ Students read the text and then listen to the trainer.

Watch out! You may need to pre-teach the following:
assume = expect
to bring someone up to speed = give someone information to make them up-to-date
anticipate = predict
hinder = not help / prevent.

Alternative

With classes that find listening difficult, ask them to listen for specific information. Write the following questions on the board (answers are shown in brackets). Students listen and answer the questions.

1 *When was Media Training Associates founded?* (2000)
2 *Who have they helped?* (more than 100 companies)
3 *How many things make a good impression?* (3)
4 *What shouldn't you assume about your audience?* (knowledge of the subject)
5 *What do you need to anticipate?* (areas of conflict or disagreement)
6 *What makes a clear structure?* (three points and a beginning and end)
7 *What makes a bad visual aid?* (packed with information, complicated diagrams, or lots of bullet points)

Watch out! Students might find it difficult to understand the difference between *manage to* and *succeed in*. They are very similar and can often be used interchangeably. However, *succeed in* is used to emphasize an achievement (*she succeeded in winning the race*), whereas *manage to* is used more generally to express ability and implies that something was difficult to do (*she managed to learn how to use the software*).

4 Students make sentences with the words in **3**.

5 70▷ Before playing the listening, discuss what is happening in the pictures. Students then listen and match.

> **Answers**
> **1** c
> **2** b
> **3** a

6 70▷ Students listen again and match the adjective + noun collocations.

> **Answers**
> complete waste of time
> absolute flop
> total disaster
> significant breakthrough
> great success
> amazing achievement
> real triumph

7 Students categorize the phrases in **6**.

> **Answers**
> **successes**: significant breakthrough, great success, amazing achievement, real triumph
> **failures**: complete waste of time, absolute flop, total disaster

Pronunciation

Explain to students that we often add emphasis to these collocations by stressing the adjective, and in particular its stressed syllable. Drill the following words with the stress:
  significant, great, amazing, real, complete, absolute, total.
Now drill the adjective with the noun to show which carries greater stress:
  e.g. *significant breakthrough.*

8 Students think of other possible adjectives + noun phrases and then use them to describe the pictures.

> **Possible answers**
> complete disaster / flop / triumph / success
> absolute disaster / triumph / waste of time

> total flop / success / waste of time
> significant achievement
> great achievement / triumph
> amazing breakthrough / success
> real disaster / achievement / flop / waste of time / success

Watch out! Note that with collocations there are generally few rules governing them. Some words simply often appear together. A good dictionary will provide collocates of a word and students should get into the habit of recording the collocations of any new word.

>> If students need more practice, go to **Practice file 16** on page 132 of the **Student's Book**.

9 Students work in pairs. Allow time for students to study their *Files*. For each event students will need to use an appropriate collocation from **6** or **8** to describe how it went.

One-to-one

The student can describe all eight events, while you ask the questions.

10 Students describe the three items and say how much of a success (or failure) each one was.

Pre-work learners

Students could describe the following instead:
- their last exam
- their last lecture
- a party or celebration they went to recently.

ⓘ Refer students to the **Interactive Workbook Glossary** for further study.

Business communication skills

1 Discuss these questions as a class.

2 71,72▷ Students listen and make notes in the table. You might need to play these twice to allow students time to write all the answers.

Answers

	Olli	Sandrine
Destination	India	Vietnam
Impressions and verdict	impressive welcome from Mr Rahman, wasting their time; the factory is chaotic and old-fashioned; need to modernize old equipment; let the current contract run and look for someone else	factory is small, but the business is dynamic and efficient; his furniture is excellent quality; if they give him support, he could become better; there were a few communication problems
Next step	make sure the rest of the orders are completed; focus on improving their systems; review the situation in a couple of months	invite Mr Tran to visit them; develop the relationship

3 72▷ Students listen and write equivalent phrases from the second listening. Again, students may need to listen twice.

Answers
1 How did it go in Vietnam?
2 I'll bring you up to date.
3 Give me an overview.
4 I was pleasantly surprised.
5 Tell me more.
6 This highlights the need to
7 I think the next step is …
8 We need to concentrate particularly on …

4 Students complete the conversations with phrases from **3**. There is often more than one possible answer.

Answers
1 How did it go
2 What makes you say that
3 What were your overall impressions
4 I was impressed with
5 Tell me more
6 highlights the need
7 need to concentrate / should focus

» If students need more practice, go to **Practice file 16** on page 132 of the **Student's Book**. Students might need to refer to the *Key expressions*.

5 Students work in pairs and take turns to report back. Allow plenty of time for students to read about their trips and prepare their reports before they begin. Refer them to the *Key expressions* to help them.

6 Students can now report back on a personal experience. If they don't want to use the suggestions, they could also talk about something like a recent exam, some charity work, or solving a problem at work.

Feedback focus

Focus on the use of expressions for giving feedback. You should also check that the listener is using suitable expressions to ask for feedback and justification.

(i) Refer students to the **Interactive Workbook Email** and **Phrasebank** sections for further study.

Practically speaking

1 Students underline the words / phrases for generalizing.

Answers
on the whole, all in all, overall, mainly, mostly, in general, generally speaking

2 73▷ Students work in pairs and make sentences. They then listen and compare their answers.

Answers from the listening
1 In general, I prefer to travel by train.
2 We mostly operate in the Far East.
3 I thought it was an excellent presentation overall.
4 Generally speaking, we don't work at weekends.
5 On the whole, it was a great trip.
6 We mainly communicate in English.
7 All in all, I was very happy with the way it went.

3 Students make sentences with the words. You could write some of the sentences below on the board as examples. As well as comparing sentences, students can ask each other further questions about their reactions.

Possible sentences
I went on a trip to India and in general it went well.
On the whole I enjoy travelling, and in particular air travel.
Mostly work's OK, although some things irritate me, especially unhelpful people.
Generally speaking my English is progressing well.
Overall it hasn't been a good year at my company, mainly because of the restructuring.

Working with words

Complete these sentences with words from the list.

| budget | track | tasks | deadline | job | updates |
| schedule | objectives | resources | skills | | |

1 We'll never meet the _____ at this rate. Can we go any faster?

2 You never know. At this speed we might even finish ahead of _____!

3 If we have another good day we'll be back on _____.

4 It's my job to allocate the necessary _____ to departments and check they have what they need.

5 The finance department is on the phone asking why we don't appear to be staying within the _____. I said they should talk to you.

6 I find delegating _____ one of the most difficult things to do on a project like this.

7 My boss likes to receive weekly _____ from everyone in order to avoid any problems or delays.

8 Any successful project needs the manager to set clear _____ right from the beginning.

9 Any project is an opportunity to learn new _____.

10 Come on everyone. Let's get on with the _____, otherwise we'll never get home.

Business communication skills

Complete these questions with the missing words.

11 _____'s everything going?

12 _____'s happening with the paint I ordered?

13 So, _____ are we with stage one?

14 _____ you call them for me and find out where the delivery is?

15 _____ don't I do that for you? I've got time.

Match answers in 16–20 to questions in 11–15. Write the question numbers next to the responses.

16 I'm afraid I'm busy. ___

17 Great. Thanks. ___

18 We've completed it. ___

19 So far so good. ___

20 We're still waiting for it. ___

Read these phrases for starting and ending a call. There is one unnecessary word in each phrase. Write this word next to the phrase.

21 Hello. Samira is speaking. _____

22 I must let you get on with. _____

23 What can I to do for you? _____

24 Thanks for your calling. _____

Language at work

Complete this email with the present simple or present continuous of the verbs in brackets.

Dear Jaime

As you know, currently Josie [25]_____ (take) a month off because of family problems. As a result, I [26]_____ (need) someone to take over her responsibilities on the New York project. So the reason I [27]_____ (email) you is to ask if you could deal with it. I [28]_____ (understand) that you are very busy at the moment, but I [29]_____ (think) I could delegate some of your less urgent work to Bruno. I called your office and they said you [30]_____ (interview) people for the new position all day, so can you call me back asap tomorrow?

Thanks.

Result _____ / 30 marks

Role cards

Copy this page and cut out the role cards for the students. Then use the *Speaking test results* forms to evaluate each student's performance. You can then cut out the results and give them to the students.

Cut along this line

Student A

You and your partner run a training company. Call your partner to get an update on a seminar for managers this weekend. You need an update on the following:

- the venue
- refreshments.

This is the current situation.

The two trainers

They have confirmed. One of them needs a hotel for the night before the seminar.

Stationery

The supplier hasn't delivered paper with the company logo on.

Decide who will deal with which tasks and by when. Remember to summarize your decisions at the end of the call.

Student B

You and your partner run a training company. Your partner calls to get an update on a seminar for managers this weekend. This is the current situation.

The venue

The original hotel has cancelled the booking so you are looking for another venue.

Refreshments

The caterers will arrive at midday.

You need an update from your partner on the following:

- the two trainers
- stationery.

Decide who will deal with which tasks and by when. Remember to summarize your decisions at the end of the call.

Cut along this line

Speaking test results

Use these forms to evaluate the students.

Cut along this line

Student A

Can the student ...	Didn't do this (0 points)	Yes, but with some mistakes (1 point)	Yes, did this very well (2 points)
start the call?			
ask for and give an update?			
offer or decline to do something?			
summarize the action needed?			
end the call?			

Result _____ / 10 marks

Student B

Can the student ...	Didn't do this (0 points)	Yes, but with some mistakes (1 point)	Yes, did this very well (2 points)
start the call?			
ask for and give an update?			
offer or decline to do something?			
summarize the action needed?			
end the call?			

Result _____ / 10 marks

Cut along this line

Working with words

Complete these adjectives with the missing letters.

1 There's a really _xc_t_n_ film on TV. Come and watch!

2 I've just sat through one of the most b_r_ _ _ presentations in my life. Everyone was nearly asleep.

3 We had a r_l_x_ _ _ break at a health spa.

4 Standing at the top of a mountain after a long hike is one the most ex_ _ _ar_t_ _ _ feelings.

5 Everyone in my office has a different background, so we have really i_ter_ _t_ _ _ conversations.

6 We have a terrible boss who tries to motivate us by making sure we're f_ _ _ht_n_ _ of losing our jobs.

7 One of the most _nj_y_ b_ _ holidays I have ever had was staying at home doing nothing. It was great!

8 The trip was really t_ _ _ _g, especially because delays at the airport added five hours to the flight.

Business communication skills

Put these words in the right order to make questions.

9 do find you how our country

_____?

10 often do they visit head how office

_____?

11 films do sort you what like of

_____?

Complete these sentences with the missing words.

12 They're interested _____ different cultures.

13 Rita is fond _____ Opera.

14 Actually, I'm not that keen _____ seafood.

15 She's simply crazy _____ skiing. She goes every winter.

16 He doesn't seem excited _____ the changes at work.

17 Anyway, I'd better get _____. Speak again later.

18 Sorry, but I should get _____ to my work now.

Read this voicemail and complete the information on the note pad (scoring = three marks in total, lose one mark per error).

Hi. Can you call me back on double oh seven, three nine three, double one oh, two nine four? Or if I'm out, you can email me at michela dash thirteen at enterprise underscore one dot F for Freddy I for Italy all lowercase.

19–21 Michela called. Call her back on _____ or email her at _____.

Language at work

Complete this conversation with the past simple or the present perfect of the verbs in brackets.

Jane Hello Samuel, [22]_____ you _____ (you / meet) Frank?

Samuel No, I haven't. Nice to meet you. Is this your first time in the US?

Frank I [23]_____ (come) here when I was a student, but that [24]_____ (be) a long time ago now!

Jane Frank works at our office in Vienna.

Samuel Oh. I'm afraid, I [25]_____ (never / be) to Austria. I've heard that the skiing is great.

Frank Yes, our family always spends some of their holidays in the mountains.

Samuel I love skiing. We're planning our next skiing trip at the moment. [26]_____ (you / ever / be) skiing in Italy, Frank?

Frank Yes, I have.

Samuel When [27]_____ (you / go)?

Frank I [28]_____ (go) about five years ago, with a group of friends. It [29]_____ (be) great there, but if you're going skiing in Europe you should definitely try Austria. I could show you around.

Samuel That sounds great!

Jane Sorry to stop you there, but we really need to go now Frank. I [30]_____ (put) you in the office next to mine.

Frank Sure, let's go. It was nice meeting you Samuel.

Result _____ / 30 marks

Role cards

Copy this page and cut out the role cards for the students. Students should do both role-plays. Then use the *Speaking test results* forms to evaluate each student's performance. You can then cut out the results and give them to the students.

Cut along this line

Student A

1 Roger Smythe is visiting your company for the first time. Call an old colleague to find out more about this client:
 • ask about work in general and his / her recent holiday
 • explain the reason for calling
 • find out the client's number and email address
 • ask about what the client likes doing in his free time
 • end the conversation.

2 You are a college professor and one of your students is doing a work placement with a company. You are an old friend of the training manager at the company. Your friend calls. Make conversation and answer questions about the student:
 • the student's email is ivonna_76@polnet.pl
 • the student is doing a thesis on marketing
 • you think she is keen on hiking and music.

Student B

1 You have just come back from holiday. An old colleague calls. Make conversation and answer questions about a client:
 • the client's number is 0044 576 847 22
 • the client's email is r_smythe@langleyhills.com
 • the client is fond of Italian food and keen on modern art.

2 You are a training manager and a student called Ivonna Pajak is coming to do a work placement at your company. Her college professor is an old friend, so you call to find out more about the student:
 • ask about work in general and about his / her family
 • explain the reason for calling
 • find out the student's email address
 • ask about what the student likes doing in her free time
 • end the conversation.

Cut along this line

Speaking test results

Use these forms to evaluate the students.

Cut along this line

Student A

Can the student …	Didn't do this (0 points)	Yes, but with some mistakes (1 point)	Yes, did this very well (2 points)
start a telephone call?			
talk about work and leisure?			
find out a person's contact details?			
find out about a person's interests?			
end a conversation?			

Result _____ / 10 marks

Student B

Can the student …	Didn't do this (0 points)	Yes, but with some mistakes (1 point)	Yes, did this very well (2 points)
start a telephone call?			
talk about work and leisure?			
find out a person's contact details?			
find out about a person's interests?			
end a conversation?			

Result _____ / 10 marks

Cut along this line

Working with words

Complete these sentences with words from the list.

immediate	user-friendly	efficient	time-saving
accurate	personal	convenient	up-to-date

1 Your home page is really easy to use. It's _____.

2 How _____ is this data? It seems to be for last month.

3 Can you give me an _____ reply on this, as I need to know straight away?

4 The new supermarket is very easy to get to from my house. It's really _____ for me.

5 These figures don't seem to be _____. I've found at least two mistakes.

6 The engine on my new car is so _____. It does more miles than my last one with the same amount of petrol.

7 We will not pass on any of your _____ details to other companies without your permission.

8 These new _____ procedures have really reduced the hours everyone spends on paperwork.

Match 9–13 to a–e.

9 Consultants help … ___

10 Call centres make it easier … ___

11 Search engines let … ___

12 Using a laptop allows … ___

13 Financial advisors help … ___

a for us to handle large numbers of enquiries.
b staff to keep working while on the move.
c us find information at the click of a button.
d us to deal with our tax payments.
e organizations to improve the way they operate.

Business communication skills

Complete these sentences with the correct prepositions.

14 It looks difficult _____ first, …

15 … but _____ fact it's easier once you know how.

16 It's user-friendly, so _____ other words, our customers will like it.

17 The purpose _____ today's meeting is to …

18 That is a downside, but _____ the plus side …

19 _____ the one hand it's more expensive, but on the other it's more efficient.

Language at work

Complete these sentences with adjectives from the list. Change the form of the adjectives if necessary.

friendly	long	complicated
convenient	stressful	fast

20 My previous job was much _____ than my present one. I feel much more relaxed now.

21 This new printer isn't nearly as _____ as the old one. You have to wait ages for it to print.

22 I'm sure you miss Sonia. How is your new assistant getting on? Is she as _____ as Sonia?

23 They say the tax system is going to be simple, but it seems _____ than ever to me.

24 My commute to work is even _____ now that they've closed the road.

25 Online banking is so much _____.

Choose the correct answer from the words in *italics*.

26 I thought this week's meeting was prepared *slightly / significantly* better than last week. It was still quite bad, but at least we had an agenda this time!

27 The new software *is nearly / isn't nearly* as complicated as the previous version. They've really improved it.

28 The more you use it, *the better / as good* you'll become.

29 We certainly work a *great / lot* deal more like a team.

30 I think a *little / few* more time spent planning might help.

Result _____ / 30 marks

Role card

This *Speaking test* has only one role card because each student has to give an individual presentation. Copy this page and cut out the role card for the student. Then use the *Speaking test results* form to evaluate the student's performance. You can then cut out the results and give them to the student.

Cut along this line

Your company wants to introduce new ways of working. You have been asked to give a presentation on hot-desking and to explain the benefits and drawbacks. Read this summary about hot-desking.

Hot-desking is a working practice where employees do not have their own desks, but they are given a workspace depending on their needs. This means that they may share a desk or workspace with other members of staff.

The benefits are that
- staff who work at different times can share space
- it makes better use of resources if staff are often out of the office.

The drawbacks are that
- staff must always clear their desks
- staff do not have a permanent place to work from
- it makes it difficult to build relationships with colleagues.

Now prepare and give your presentation.

Remember to
- introduce your presentation
- explain how the system works
- explain the advantages and disadvantages
- compare it with the current system.

Cut along this line

Speaking test results

Use this form to evaluate the student.

Cut along this line

Can the student ...	Didn't do this (0 points)	Yes, but with some mistakes (1 point)	Yes, did this very well (2 points)
introduce the purpose of the presentation?			
explain how the system works?			
explain the benefits?			
explain any drawbacks?			
compare it with the current system?			

Result _____ / 10 marks

Cut along this line

Working with words

Complete these sentences with words from the list. Change the form of the word if necessary.

guarantee	require	assist	provide
serve	monitor	care	satisfy	expect

1 Can you _____ that the package will arrive within 24 hours?

2 The _____ was rather slow at that new restaurant, but the food was good when it arrived.

3 As part of your fitness check, we attach this machine to your chest and it allows us to _____ your heart.

4 In a recent survey we found that callers' levels of _____ with the call centre were below average.

5 With over 300 products in stock, we're sure you'll find something to meet your _____.

6 We not only want to meet the _____ of our customers, we also want to exceed them.

7 I asked the shop _____ for help, but she was very rude to me.

8 Our customer _____ policy is there to ensure your complete satisfaction.

9 What kind of after-sales support does your company _____ for its customers?

Business communication skills

Complete this conversation with the missing words.

A Hello, I'm interested 10_____ your advert for customer service staff. Can you tell me a 11_____ more about the position?

B Sure, we have part-time and full-time vacancies and basically you answer questions and help customers with any problems. Is that something you could deal 12_____?

A Yes, I think so. I'd also like to find out 13_____ the pay.

B Well, it would depend on your experience. The best idea is for you to come in for a chat. Would it be 14_____ for you to do that?

A Maybe.

B 15_____ about sometime this week?

A Next week would be better.

B OK. Wednesday the second 16_____ me.

A Sorry, I can't 17_____ Wednesday, but I'm free on Thursday afternoon.

B That's fine …

Later the same day, the person calls again. Complete this conversation with the missing words.

A Hello, I called earlier about the post in customer service and we arranged an interview for next Thursday afternoon.

B Oh yes. I remember.

A Well, I'm very sorry, but can we 18_____ it forward to the morning?

B Well, I'm quite busy on Thursday morning. I'd 19_____ the Friday morning.

A That's fine. 10 o'clock is 20_____ for me.

B Fine. We'll see you then …

Language at work

Confirm a meeting with a customer by email. Write each line of the email using the words below (two marks per sentence).

21 write – confirm – our meeting – Friday 4th

22 we – meet – 10 a.m. – my office

23 bus to our company – leave – from train station – every fifteen minutes

24 please note – our head of sales – also – join – us

25 look forward – see – you

21 _____

22 _____

23 _____

24 _____

25 _____

Result _____ / 30 marks

Role cards

Copy this page and cut out the role cards for the students. Students should do both role-plays. Then use the *Speaking test results* forms to evaluate each student's performance. You can then cut out the results and give them to the students.

Cut along this line

Student A

1 You need a venue for your company's annual Sales convention. Call a hotel in Dallas and find out about
• location (distance to stations, airports)
• number of rooms
• meeting rooms
• relaxation facilities.

Arrange a meeting. You are busy on 26th May (p.m.) and 27th May. You are free on 28th May (p.m.)

2 You manage a conference centre in Zurich. Answer a call.
Hotel location: twelve minutes from airport, fifteen minutes from train station.
Centre facilities: main room has seating for 1,500, twenty lecture rooms (50–200 per room), bars, two restaurants.
Audio-visual: projectors, audio, and flexible seating.

Arrange a meeting. You are free on 3rd March (p.m.) and 5th March (a.m.). You are busy on 1st, 2nd (a.m.), and 4th March.

Student B

1 You manage a hotel in Dallas which often hosts conventions for businesses. Answer a call.

Hotel location: 30 minutes from airport, ten minutes from train station.
Number of rooms: 200.
Meeting rooms: one main room with 300 seat capacity, twenty seminar rooms.
Relaxation facilities: pool, sauna, fitness gym, and restaurant.

Arrange a meeting. You are free on 26th May (p.m.) and 28th May. You are busy on 25th and 27th May.

2 You are looking for a conference centre in Switzerland. Call a centre in Zurich and find out about
• location (distance to stations, airports)
• size / rooms / refreshments
• audio-visual facilities.

Arrange a meeting. You are busy on 2nd March (p.m.). You are free on 1st, 3rd (p.m.), 4th (a.m.), and 5th March.

Cut along this line

Speaking test results

Use these forms to evaluate the students.

Cut along this line

Student A

Can the student ...	Didn't do this (0 points)	Yes, but with some mistakes (1 point)	Yes, did this very well (2 points)
explain purpose of the call?			
ask for all the information?			
suggest times for a meeting?			
make an appointment?			
end the call?			

Result _____ / 10

Student B

Can the student ...	Didn't do this (0 points)	Yes, but with some mistakes (1 point)	Yes, did this very well (2 points)
explain purpose of the call?			
ask for all the information?			
suggest times for a meeting?			
make an appointment?			
end the call?			

Result _____ / 10

Cut along this line

Working with words

Complete these sentences with words from the list. Note that one word cannot be used.

trip	facilities	journey	travel	venues	check

1 How did your business _____ go? Was it successful?

2 I don't mind a long _____ on a plane if it's comfortable and there aren't any delays.

3 Have they confirmed all their _____ arrangements with us? For example, when are they arriving?

4 Why don't you _____ in online, rather than waiting at the airport?

5 The _____ at that airport are excellent for business travellers. They even provide secretarial services.

Complete these words with the missing letters.

6 This is a local spe_____ cooked in olive oil.

7 What kind of entert_____ do you think they would enjoy? Perhaps opera? Or a play?

8 There's a weekend exc_____ to Sicily which you might enjoy while you're here.

9 When you travel as much as I do, visiting old castles, museums, and sigh_____ is fairly tiring to be honest.

10 Thank you so much for your hosp_____. Everyone's been so kind to me.

11 I hear the ni_____ is good in Barcelona. Let's go out tonight and see if it's true.

Choose the correct answer from the words in *italics*.

12 Would you like to freshen *out / up / off* before dinner?

13 I will pick Mr Hayes *off / out / up* from the hotel.

14 He needed more time to show them *up / around / for* the factory, so I guess they're still there.

15 You will need to check *out / in / on* at reception when you arrive, and then join us in the bar.

16 One thing I'd like to do while I'm here is to meet *along / up / on* with an old friend who lives in the centre of town.

17 How about eating *in / out / with* at that restaurant?

Business communication skills

Match 18–24 to a response in a–h. Write the letters after the sentences. Note that one response cannot be used.

18 Did you have any trouble finding us? ____

19 It's nice to meet you in person. ____

20 Can I get you a coffee? ____

21 Let me take your coat. ____

22 We're going to begin with a tour of the technical centre. ____

23 For your safety, don't touch the machinery. ____

24 We'll catch up again after lunch. ____

a No, not really.
b That sounds good. Let's go.
c It's fine thanks.
d Great. See you then.
e I'll hang on to it for now.
f Thanks. White, please.
g Sure. No problem.
h Likewise.

Language at work

Complete this conversation with verbs from the list.

don't need	have to	allowed
supposed	need	mustn't

A OK. The first thing to remember is that you
25_____ log on, so you'll always
26_____ to remember your password.

B I heard that they change the passwords every month.

A IT is 27_____ to reset them, but often don't do it. OK, once you've typed it in, wait a few seconds while the system opens. You 28_____ click anything, or it all crashes.

B I see. By the way, am I 29_____ to send personal emails? Or is that against the rules?

A No, you 30_____ to worry too much, but you mustn't download any unknown documents.

Result _____ / 30 marks

Role cards

Copy this page and cut out the role cards for the students. Students should do both role-plays. Then use the *Speaking test results* forms to evaluate each student's performance. You can then cut out the results and give them to the students.

Cut along this line

Student A

1 You are meeting a visitor to your factory, which produces computer components. The schedule for today is as follows.

Morning: tour of the factory
Lunch: meet the head of production
Afternoon: visit the technical centre (10 kilometres away)

- Welcome the visitor who has flown in this morning.
- Ask about the journey and offer something to drink.
- Remember to explain the reasons for wearing overalls and not touching any components in the factory area.

2 You are visiting a brand new conference centre in Milan to decide if it will be suitable for a three-day conference. You travelled overnight by train from Zurich.
- Meet your host. You'd like to start the tour straight away.
- Ask about the schedule and mention that you'd also like to do some shopping later in the day, if you have time.

Student B

1 You are visiting a factory which produces computer components. You have a two-hour flight and short taxi ride from the airport to the factory.
- Meet your hosts. You'd like to start the tour straight away.
- Ask about the schedule and explain that you would also like to meet Dr Ruth Obach, who is in charge of research and development.

2 You are in charge of a new conference centre in Milan. You are meeting a potential client, who has travelled overnight from Zurich. The schedule for today is as follows.

Morning: tour the main seminar rooms of the centre
Lunch: eat out at a nearby local restaurant
Afternoon: visit the newly built hotel connected to the centre

- Meet and welcome the visitor.
- Ask about the journey and offer something to drink.
- Remember to explain that the visitor needs to wear an identity pass at all times.

Cut along this line

Speaking test results

Use these forms to evaluate the students.

Cut along this line

Student A

Can the student ...	Didn't do this (0 points)	Yes, but with some mistakes (1 point)	Yes, did this very well (2 points)
welcome the visitor?			
ask about the journey?			
offer a drink?			
talk about the schedule?			
remind the visitor about safety?			

Result _____ / 10 marks

Student B

Can the student ...	Didn't do this (0 points)	Yes, but with some mistakes (1 point)	Yes, did this very well (2 points)
welcome the visitor?			
ask about the journey?			
offer a drink?			
talk about the schedule?			
remind the visitor about safety?			

Result _____ / 10 marks

Cut along this line

Working with words

Complete these sentences with words from the list.

| breach | prevent | access | pass | monitor |
| security | safeguard | safety | password | |

1 Call health and _____ and tell them someone has been injured in production!

2 What _____ measures are you planning for the arrival of the President?

3 Don't tell me they've changed the _____ again for this computer, have they?

4 There was a _____ of security at our plant in Bristol. Someone cut a hole in the fence and broke in.

5 It keeps saying 'Unauthorized _____. Re-enter PIN', but I'm using my normal PIN number.

6 Excuse me, may I see your _____ please?

7 This new software didn't _____ us from getting that virus. Are you sure it's a good product?

8 In order to _____ against problems of identity theft, the card has a special chip.

9 By having CCTV, the company is able to _____ for unauthorized personnel on site.

Business communication skills

Replace 10–18 in the dialogue with a–i, so that the meaning stays the same. Write the letters next to the numbers.

10 ___   11 ___   12 ___   13 ___   14 ___
15 ___   16 ___   17 ___   18 ___

a as it stands
b up to now
c are aware
d do you mean
e if I understand you correctly
f update you on
g follow you
h by having
i what's the reason for

A As you [10]*know*, we've recently had a visit from a security consultant and I'd like to [11]*tell you about* their findings. They advise that we install sprinkler systems. The situation [12]*now* is that we only have fire alarms. The building would be safer in the event of a fire [13]*because of* the sprinklers.

Secondly, [14]*so far* we've always had security staff in reception, but not in the car park. We now plan to have security at the entrance.

B Sorry, I'm not sure I [15]*understand*. [16]*Are you saying* we'll have to show our ID badges to get into the car park?

A Yes, that's right.

B [17]*Why are we doing* that?

A It's because anyone can drive in at the moment.

B So, [18]*you mean that* we'll have to stop, show our badge, and then show it again when we walk in. It'll take ages!

Language at work

Complete these sentences with the present perfect simple or present perfect continuous of the verbs in brackets.

A [19]_____ (you / hear) the news?

B What [20]_____ (happen)?

A Richard [21]_____ (resign)!

B You're kidding! Why?

A They say he [22]_____ (steal) stationery regularly for some time now.

B Really? Do they know exactly how long he [23]_____ (do) that?

A No one knows for sure.

B I don't believe it. I work with him every day and I [24]_____ (never / see) him take anything. And anyway, why [25]_____ (they / not / fire) him if that's true?

A I don't know. They [26]_____ (talk) to him all afternoon, so maybe we'll find out before we leave tonight.

Choose the correct answer from the words in *italics*.

27 It's the second attachment with a virus this week. *Consequently / Due to*, we'll scan everything.

28 *In order to / So that* there's no delay, I've asked her to contact them straight away.

29 Make a backup disk *so / therefore* you don't lose files.

30 We'll have to increase the number of security staff *because of / in order that* these changes.

Result _____ / 30 marks

Speaking test

Role cards

Copy this page and cut out the role cards for the students. Students should do both role-plays. Then use the *Speaking test results* forms to evaluate each student's performance. You can then cut out the results and give them to the students.

Cut along this line

Student A

1 You manage a small office of five people. You want to change the lunch break system. Give a presentation on the situation.

   Present situation: all staff take lunch at the same time.
   Problem: there is no one in the office over lunch and clients have complained about this.
   Proposed changes: staff will take lunch at different times; lunch will begin at 11.30 a.m. for some and 12.30 p.m. for others.

   Be prepared to answer questions!

2 You work for a small, but growing company. The owner wants to propose a change.

   You think he wants to make Sandra Piaf the new manager. You are not happy about the change. You think staff can work on their own when the owner is away (and you don't like Sandra).

   Listen to the presentation and ask questions.

Student B

1 You work in a small office of five people. Your manager wants to propose changes to the lunch break system.

   You are not happy about the changes, especially the proposal that some lunch breaks will begin at 11.30 a.m.

   Listen to the presentation and ask questions.

2 You own a small, but growing business. You want to appoint an assistant to be in charge when you are away. Give a short presentation on the situation.

   Present situation: you have to travel more and more and you will be employing three more staff next month.
   Problem: no one is in charge when you are away and you also need an assistant to help with the growing business.
   Proposed changes: appoint Sandra Piaf (a current employee) to be your assistant; all staff will report to her when you are away.

   Be prepared to answer questions!

Cut along this line

Speaking test results

Use these forms to evaluate the students.

Cut along this line

Student A

Can the student ...	Didn't do this (0 points)	Yes, but with some mistakes (1 point)	Yes, did this very well (2 points)
give background to the situation?			
explain problems?			
propose changes?			
answer questions?			
convince the other person?			

Result _____ / 10 marks

Student B

Can the student ...	Didn't do this (0 points)	Yes, but with some mistakes (1 point)	Yes, did this very well (2 points)
give background to the situation?			
explain problems?			
propose changes?			
answer questions?			
convince the other person?			

Result _____ / 10 marks

Cut along this line

Working with words

Complete these words with the missing letters.

1 You should take more r_ _p_ _ _ _ _ _ _ _y at work – that way you might get promoted.

2 We're too similar. We have the same strengths. Our skills aren't c_ m_ _ _ _ _ _t_ _y.

3 Maybe we should join f_r_ _s and find a solution together.

4 The two companies are hoping to form an a_l_ _ _ _e in order to survive this current recession.

5 Nigel isn't much of a team p_a_ _r, I'm afraid. He prefers to work alone.

6 Let's start by finding some common g_o_ _d, rather than focusing on our disagreements.

7 I'd like you two to work more c_o_ _ _y together in the future.

8 It's a joint v_n_ _ _e between a coffee company and an electronics firm to produce vending machines.

Business communication skills

Complete these sentences with phrases from the list.

next step	chances are	well done	going to
the deadline	intend to	I expect	likely that
planned to	timescale on		

A So, what's the 9_____?

B Well I 10_____ talk to the client and get some feedback. It's 11_____ they'll ask us to speed the project up.

A Remind me. What's the 12_____ this?

B July 31st is 13_____, but they'd like July 1st.

A That's rather optimistic.

B Well, I'm 14_____ need more people, but I expect we'll be OK. I've 15_____ employ more freelance staff anyway, so it won't affect my budget.

A 16_____! That's a really good idea.

B And the 17_____ we won't be ready in time anyway, so 18_____ the final date will still be the 31st.

Complete these sentences with the correct prepositions.

19 _____ the long run it's for the best.

20 Do you think you'll be able to finish this _____ the end of the month?

21 _____ the next few weeks I intend to talk to all staff about this.

22 We'll have finished _____ next Tuesday at the latest.

23 There may be some complaints _____ the short term.

24 We plan to be ready _____ schedule.

Language at work

Choose the correct answer from the words in *italics*.

25 You *should / 're going to* come along if you have time. The CEO will be there.

26 Profits *will / might* definitely fall a little next quarter. Don't worry. They always go back up around Christmas.

27 Look at the awful findings on customer feedback. They're terrible. I think we *should / 're going to* lose some of our key clients based on this report.

28 I'm not 100% sure, but I think I *might / will* apply for that job in the paper.

29 Let me check with the warehouse, and then I promise that I *'ll / 'm going to* call you straight back.

30 There's usually a shuttle bus that leaves the conference centre at 3 p.m. If it's running today there *is going to / should* be one in about five minutes.

Result _____ / 30 marks

Speaking test

Role cards

Copy this page and cut out the role cards for the students. Students should do both role-plays. Then use the *Speaking test results* forms to evaluate each student's performance. You can then cut out the results and give them to the students.

Cut along this line

Student A

1 You work in the human resources department of a very large car factory. The production manager needs fifteen new trainee employees in September. It is the end of May.

Your production manager calls. Explain your plan and timescale.

Plan: advertise at local technical colleges; hold open days and visits for students; interview students; get references from lecturers.
Hopes and expectations: recruit by end of July; avoid expensive advertising.

2 You are the managing director of a medium-sized firm.

Call the sales manager for an update on this year's brochure and price list. You want it ready for October 1st and it is now September 2nd. Find out from your sales manager the timescale for this.

Student B

1 You are the production manager at a very large car factory and you need fifteen new trainee employees in September. It is the end of May.

Call the head of human resources to find out his / her plan and intentions for recruitment. Remember to find out about the timescale for this.

2 You are the sales manager for a medium-sized firm.

Your managing director calls for an update on this year's brochure and price list. It is due for October 1st and it is now September 2nd. Explain your plan and timescale.

Plan: contact the designers; contact the printers; hold a meeting to discuss prices for the year.
Hopes and expectations: there will be a delay because we need new photographs of products; it's going to be a few days late.

Cut along this line

Speaking test results

Use these forms to evaluate the students.

Cut along this line

Student A

Can the student ...	Didn't do this (0 points)	Yes, but with some mistakes (1 point)	Yes, did this very well (2 points)
answer the call?			
describe plans and intentions?			
express hopes and expectations?			
explain timescale?			
end the call?			

Result _____ / 10 marks

Student B

Can the student ...	Didn't do this (0 points)	Yes, but with some mistakes (1 point)	Yes, did this very well (2 points)
answer the call?			
describe plans and intentions?			
express hopes and expectations?			
explain timescale?			
end the call?			

Result _____ / 10 marks

Cut along this line

Working with words

Choose the correct answer from the words in *italics*.

1 We don't need to store any *components / warehouse* on site because they are delivered when we need them.

2 It's possible to keep a constant check on the *supply chain / inventory* using bar codes.

3 There's a *customer / supplier* on the phone complaining about a late payment again.

4 Everything is *streamlined / distributed* to our retailers using private logistics firms.

5 One way to ensure quality is to begin by checking the *rough / raw* materials that we buy in.

Complete these sentences with the missing words.

6 You should give them a call and find out where our order is. We don't want to run _____ again like last time and be left with nothing.

7 How _____ are we running on replacement mother boards?

8 I've called three places now and they all say they are _____ of stock.

9 If you log on to the site, you type in this reference number and it'll keep track _____ your order.

10 For this party I think we'll need to stock up _____ more of that chocolate ice cream. It was really popular last time and went within five minutes!

11 You're in luck. We have one left _____ stock. How would you like it delivered?

Business communication skills

Complete this conversation with words from the list.

place	look	problem	following	find
according	put	asap	take	

A Compusource components. Linda speaking.
B Hello, this is Kris Triers. I'm ¹²_____ up an order I made three weeks ago. I'd like to ¹³_____ out about it.

A Sure. Can I ¹⁴_____ your account details?
B Yes, the reference number was UU-1100.
A OK. Let me see. When did you ¹⁵_____ the order exactly?
B The 4th of March I think.
A OK. Was that fifty sound cards?
B That's right.
A OK, Mr Triers. ¹⁶_____ to my information, these were ¹⁷_____ through to the warehouse on the 10th of March.
B But I asked for them to be sent ¹⁸_____. Are you sure? This is a real ¹⁹_____ for us.
A I'll ²⁰_____ into it immediately. Will you hold?
B Sure.

Complete these sentences with the correct prepositions.

21 Please charge it _____ my account.

22 Could you check it _____ for me?

23 It was dispatched _____ Monday.

24 I'm not happy _____ this.

25 I've had enough _____ this.

26 I'll get back _____ you.

Language at work

Read this voicemail message. Then complete the note to your boss using reported speech.

'Hi, it's Peter. Just calling to say I've looked into the problem and our warehouse manager tells me they sent the items two days ago. Can you call me when they arrive?'

Message: Peter called. He said
27_____ the problem and
the warehouse manager 28_____
they 29_____ the items
two days ago. He 30_____
him when they arrive.

Result _____ / 30 marks

Role cards

Copy this page and cut out the role cards for the students. Students should do both role-plays. Then use the *Speaking test results* forms to evaluate each student's performance. You can then cut out the results and give them to the students.

Cut along this line

Student A

1 Call your computer supplier:
   - identify yourself
   - give reason for calling
   - place an order for 100 motherboards
   - check where the delivery from last month is (ref no: RG566)
   - complain about the problem
   - give contact number for supplier to call you back on.

2 You are a stationery supplier:
   - answer Student B's call
   - take the order
   - ask for details of late order
   - explain that it was sent to the wrong customer
   - promise action.

Student B

1 You are a computer supplier:
   - answer Student A's call
   - take the order
   - ask for details of late order
   - explain that it was sent by ship not air
   - promise action.

2 Call your stationery supplier:
   - identify yourself
   - give reason for calling
   - place an order for 200 folders
   - check where the delivery from last month is (ref no: EA-1001)
   - complain about the problem
   - give contact number for supplier to call you back on.

Cut along this line

Speaking test results

Use these forms to evaluate the students.

Cut along this line

Student A

Can the student ...	Didn't do this (0 points)	Yes, but with some mistakes (1 point)	Yes, did this very well (2 points)
identify him / herself and give reason for call?			
place the order?			
check previous delivery?			
complain?			
give contact number?			

Result _____ / 10 marks

Student B

Can the student ...	Didn't do this (0 points)	Yes, but with some mistakes (1 point)	Yes, did this very well (2 points)
identify him / herself and give reason for call?			
place the order?			
check previous delivery?			
complain?			
give contact number?			

Result _____ / 10 marks

Cut along this line

Working with words

Choose the correct answer from the words in _italics_.

1 We are still _badly equipped / cramped_. There simply isn't enough space for anyone to work.

2 I made all the changes we discussed, so the reports are now _state-of-the-art / up-to-date_.

3 The old warehouses are quite _run out / run down_. Should we renovate them or build new ones?

4 Everything's new here. Even the water-cooler! So we're about as _well equipped / spacious_ as you can be.

Which intensifier _cannot_ be used in each sentence?

5 How was your weekend?
— quiet, actually. I just read and watched TV. And you?
a Fairly   **b** Quite   **c** Not very

6 This isn't ___ what I had in mind, but never mind. It should be OK.
a exactly   **b** quite   **c** fairly

7 The new Jaguar has a / an ___ powerful engine. It does 0–60 in five seconds.
a very   **b** exactly   **c** extremely

8 The new offices aren't ___ easy to find. You need to turn right off the motorway.
a very   **b** exactly   **c** pretty

Business communication skills

Complete these questions with the missing words.

9 _____ about installing new phones?

10 _____ don't we ask them to give their comments?

11 _____ you thought about introducing bonuses?

12 _____n't we have an open plan office area instead?

Complete these sentences with words from the list.

| maybe   work   sure   consider   prove |
| reservations   better   worth   rather |

13 _____ we should begin by brainstorming a few ideas.

14 It might _____ more difficult than we think.

15 I really think we should _____ a few more options.

16 We might be _____ off going to another supplier.

17 It's probably _____ seeing what staff think first.

18 I have some _____ about that proposal.

19 I'd _____ not bring in any more freelancers if at all possible.

20 Sorry, but I don't think that would _____.

21 I'm not entirely _____.

Language at work

Match 22–30 to a–i.

22 There isn't a lot … ___

23 There are some … ___

24 You don't have much … ___

25 Only a … ___

26 A few … ___

27 We don't think many customers … ___

28 I'm sorry, but I don't have … ___

29 There aren't many people … ___

30 How … ___

a any paper clips left.
b left at the old headquarters now.
c of extra time, so your schedule must be right.
d employees would like a smoking room.
e running machines at the back.
f space in here, do you?
g much of the day is spent in meetings?
h little money gets wasted using this system.
i care about quality, as long as the price is low.

Result _____ / 30 marks

Speaking test

Role card

This *Speaking test* has only one role card because each student has to give an individual presentation. Copy this page and cut out the role card for the student. Then use the *Speaking test results* form to evaluate the student's performance. You can then cut out the results and give them to the student.

Cut along this line

- -

Prepare and give a mini-presentation. Follow these stages:
- introduce and describe the place where you work (style of office, atmosphere, current facilities)
- explain the advantages of the work place
- explain any disadvantages
- recommend two possible improvements
- be prepared to answer any questions on your presentation.

Cut along this line

- -

Speaking test results

Use this form to evaluate the student.

Cut along this line

- -

Student A

Can the student ...	Didn't do this (0 points)	Yes, but with some mistakes (1 point)	Yes, did this very well (2 points)
describe his / her place of work?			
explain the advantages of the work place?			
explain any disadvantages?			
recommend two possible improvements?			
answer any questions on the topic?			

Result _____ / 10 marks

Cut along this line

- -

Working with words

Complete these sentences with words from the list. Change the form of the word if necessary.

| put | have | make | carry | have |
| reach | make | avoid | express | go |

1 Do you _____ an idea of how long they'll be?

2 Do you mind if I _____ a suggestion?

3 Why don't we _____ for this plan and see what happens?

4 I asked you to _____ out my decision and you ignored me. Why?

5 Haven't they _____ an agreement yet? It's been hours.

6 I'd like to _____ forward an idea to change how decisions are made.

7 I just can't _____ up my mind on this one.

8 Let's make sure everybody has a chance to _____ their say.

9 I know this is a sensitive issue, so let's try to _____ any confrontation during our discussion.

10 We need an environment where employees feel able to _____ their opinions freely.

Complete these words with the missing letters.

11 We'll need the full ba_ _ _ _ _ of the board for this plan. Without their support, it won't work.

12 Are you all in fa_ _ _ _ of this solution? Or are you against it?

13 The ma_ _ _ _ _ _ of the shareholders are against investing any more money into this division. Only one or two of them want to give any more money.

14 I suggest we br_ _ _ _ _ _ _ _ a few ideas and see where we end up. OK?

15 We tried reaching a co_ _ _ _ _ _ _ _, but they weren't willing to lower the price.

Business communication skills

There is one incorrect word in each phrase. Underline it and write the correct word at the end.

16 From my opinion of view it's a bad idea. _____

17 As near as I'm concerned, it's fine. _____

18 I'm not quite sure for that. _____

19 I listen what you're saying, but it won't work. _____

20 You're absolutely right. I couldn't agree much. _____

21 To be truth, I don't see how we're going to persuade them. _____

22 I have your point about the costs, but I think it's worth it. _____

23 Let's see it, he's too old for the job! _____

Language at work

Choose the correct answer from the words in *italics*.

Hi Jeff

Thanks for your advice. If you [24]*will / could* answer one or two more questions about our idea, I'd be really grateful. First of all, if we choose your idea of going online (and I think we probably [25]*will / would*), what [26]*will / would* the start up costs be – approximately? Would you know the name of someone who could design a site if we [27]*need / needed* help with this? If we could, it [28]*will / would* be fun to try and design it ourselves, but maybe that's a bad idea. What [29]*will / would* you do in our situation?

I look forward to hearing from you. If it's OK with you, I [30]*will / would* give you a call next week so that we can talk about this some more.

Best wishes
Ilse

Result _____ / 30 marks

Role card

This *Speaking test* has only one role card because students work together and have a meeting. Copy this page and cut out the role card for pairs of students. Then use the *Speaking test results* forms to evaluate each student's performance. You can then cut out the results and give them to the student.

Cut along this line

Work in pairs.

Situation:
- you all work together for a small high street shop which sells ethnic and health food
- you have been open a month and business is OK, but not great
- you live in a traditional town, so your products are quite new.

Hold a meeting to discuss ways to promote the shop locally. Discuss each of the following ideas and try to suggest others. Note that you have the budget for only two ideas. Make sure you reach a final decision.

1 Put balloons outside the shop and someone can walk around with a sign.
2 Sponsor a local event or charity.
3 Advertise in the local newspaper and ask them to write an article about you.
4 Run free cookery lessons in the shop to show people how to use the food.
5 Any other ideas?

Cut along this line

Speaking test results

Use these forms to evaluate the students.

Cut along this line

Student A

Can the student ...	Didn't do this (0 points)	Yes, but with some mistakes (1 point)	Yes, did this very well (2 points)
give opinions?			
agree / disagree?			
acknowledge what someone else says?			
check understanding?			
reach a decision?			

Result _____ / 10 marks

Student B

Can the student ...	Didn't do this (0 points)	Yes, but with some mistakes (1 point)	Yes, did this very well (2 points)
give opinions?			
agree / disagree?			
acknowledge what someone else says?			
check understanding?			
reach a decision?			

Result _____ / 10 marks

Cut along this line

Working with words

Choose the correct answer from the words in *italics*.

1 I've never seen a product like this before. It's really *reliable / original*!

2 How did you come *up / out* with that idea? It's great.

3 My new car design is only at the *brainchild / prototype* stage at present. It still needs a lot of work.

4 When I first started in business I had lots of *obstacles / catalysts* to get past because I didn't have a lot of qualifications.

5 This new mobile contains highly *reliable / sophisticated* technology. It's state-of-the-art!

6 We're a *revolutionary / traditional* company with a long history of providing quality clothes to older customers.

7 Sorry, but I don't think I follow the basic *concept / a-ha moment* for your idea.

8 He's a young, *simple / dynamic* executive with a great future!

Business communication skills

Complete this presentation with phrases a–g.

a morning and
b First
c we'll look at
d you can see
e take your questions
f let's look
g I'd like to begin

Good ⁹_____ thanks for coming. ¹⁰_____ by outlining the aim of this meeting. ¹¹_____ , I'll give an overview of the current situation with regard to staff organization. Then, ¹²_____ our proposal for some changes, and finally I'll ¹³_____ . So, ¹⁴_____ at this slide. As ¹⁵_____ , it shows you …

Replace the <u>underlined</u> phrases with a–f. Write the letters next to the numbers.

16 _____   17 _____   18 _____
19 _____   20 _____   21 _____

a couldn't hear you
b see what you mean
c get back to you on that
d 's everything I want to say
e Are there
f listening

A So that ¹⁶<u>brings me to the end of my presentation</u>. Thanks for ¹⁷<u>your attention</u>. ¹⁸<u>Do you have</u> any questions?

B Yes, how does this affect our department?

A Sorry, I ¹⁹<u>didn't catch that</u>.

B Our department. What changes does it mean?

A Good question, but can I ²⁰<u>explain that later</u>? I don't want to go into exact detail here and now.

B But I think everyone needs to hear.

A Sure, and I ²¹<u>understand your opinion</u>, but I want to be able to give you precise figures when I have them.

Language at work

Complete these sentences with the superlative form of the adjectives in the list.

well known	happy	high	valuable
bad	low	late	friendly	expensive

22 Resigning from my job was probably the _____ decision I've ever made.

23 The _____ mistake we made was investing in that company. We lost so much money.

24 I think Ireland is one of the _____ countries I've ever visited. Everyone is so nice!

25 I'd say that your employees are your _____ asset by far.

26 You got the second _____ sales results in the division. Well done!

27 Unemployment has fallen to its _____ point in ten years. Most people can get a job nowadays.

28 R&D have sent over the designs for their _____ prototype. I hope this one works!

29 Disney is probably _____ for its films for children.

30 The team seem _____ when they have clear aims and objectives.

Result _____ / 30 marks

Role card

This *Speaking test* has only one role card because each student has to give an individual presentation. Copy this page and cut out the role card for the student. Then use the *Speaking test results* form to evaluate the student's performance. You can then cut out the results and give them to the student. The student will need pens and paper to prepare a visual aid.

Cut along this line

You are in charge of creating a new mission statement for your place of work (or study).

1 Prepare your new mission statement and write it out. It should be no more than twenty words.

2 Now prepare and give a short (five-minute) presentation. Follow these three stages:
  • give a brief overview of your place of work (or study)
  • explain what you want to emphasize about it in the mission statement
  • present the final mission statement (prepare a visual aid with the mission statement written on it).

Don't forget to begin and end your presentation appropriately, and be prepared for questions at the end!

Make sure you prepare a visual aid with the mission statement written on it for the final stage.

Cut along this line

Speaking test results

Use this form to evaluate the student.

Cut along this line

Student A

Can the student …	Didn't do this (0 points)	Yes, but with some mistakes (1 point)	Yes, did this very well (2 points)
start the presentation?			
give an overview?			
refer to visuals?			
close the presentation?			
respond to questions or comments?			

Result _____ / 10 marks

Cut along this line

Working with words

Choose the correct answer from the words in *italics*.

1 Excuse me, I think there's a *fault / failure* with my washing machine.

2 Your idea's good, but there's one major *flaw / faulty* in the plan. You haven't considered what the union will say.

3 I'm sorry, but there seems to have been some kind of *breakdown / misunderstanding*. My appointment is at 2.00 p.m., and your appointment is 2.30 p.m., so I should go first.

4 Sorry, you'll have to wait if you want to use the Internet. The server will be *wrong / down* for at least three hours.

5 Don't bother trying to use that software on a PC. It's *incompatible / defective* with anything but a Mac.

6 You won't believe this. My car *is down / has broken down* for the third time this month. It's at the garage now.

7 I wouldn't use them. They'll fix it for you, but they're so *unreliable / defective* for getting things done on time.

8 Take the stairs. The lift's *down / out of order* again.

9 I think the problems are due to the *mistake / failure* of staff to communicate properly. We need some more staff training.

10 It's not always in our interests to achieve zero *failures / defective*, as this can be expensive and push up prices.

Business communication skills

Complete these conversations with the missing words.

A So what's the ^{11}m _____ exactly?
B It's this DVD. It ^{12}k _____ on switching off.
A When you say it switches off, do you ^{13}m _____ it stops, or there's no power at all?
B No power. It goes dark.
A Are you using it on battery, or mains?
B Battery I think.
A Have you ^{14}t _____ plugging in the power cable?
B Is there one?

A What appears to be the ^{15}t _____?
B My boss is ^{16}a _____ giving me more projects when we haven't finished the last ones. I just can't keep up.
A It ^{17}m _____ be useful to talk to her.
B But she's never here. I just get notes stuck on yet more reports.
A The ^{18}b _____ thing would be to ring her. Just talking should solve the problem.

A Hello, how can I ^{19}h _____?
B Well I bought this from you last week, but it doesn't work.
A What's wrong with it ^{20}e _____?
B It won't come on, and there's a smell when you plug it in.
A What ^{21}s _____ of smell?
B A kind of burning.
A It sounds ^{22}l _____ there's a problem with the electrics. I'll give you another one.

Language at work

Tick (✓) the correct sentences and change the incorrect sentences.

23 I think you should to ask for help.

_____

24 You have to get it approved by your boss.

_____

25 I'd speak to her if I would be you.

_____

26 What would you do in this situation?

_____

27 Is it enough easy for you?

_____

28 Sorry, but I don't have enough time for that.

_____

29 This is really too complicated to fix.

_____

30 The main problem is that we don't have too resources.

_____

Result _____ **/ 30 marks**

Speaking test

Role cards

Copy this page and cut out the role cards for the students. Students should do both role-plays. Then use the *Speaking test results* forms to evaluate each student's performance. You can then cut out the results and give them to the students.

Cut along this line

Student A

1 Call customer services at a computer supplier.
   Main problem: you bought a faulty computer.
   Details: you loaded some old software on to it, but it won't work with this computer; you'd like to send the computer back and get a refund.

2 Your colleague calls you with a problem. Answer the call and do the following:
   - find out the main problem and details
   - note that the problem is probably just a simple misunderstanding
   - advise your colleague to talk with his / her boss
   - confirm that better communication is the solution.

Student B

1 You work at the call centre for a computer supplier. Answer a call and do the following:
   - find out the main problem and details
   - note that there is nothing wrong with the computer, the customer's software sounds out-of-date and incompatible
   - advise the customer to buy new software
   - the company has a no refund policy.

2 Call a colleague.
   Main problem: your boss is always giving you work.
   Details: you have three reports to complete and have now been given another; your boss is never here.

Cut along this line

Speaking test results

Use these forms to evaluate the students.

Cut along this line

Student A

Can the student …	Didn't do this (0 points)	Yes, but with some mistakes (1 point)	Yes, did this very well (2 points)
ask what the problem is?			
ask for details?			
diagnose the problem?			
give advice?			
confirm a solution?			

Result _____ / 10 marks

Student B

Can the student …	Didn't do this (0 points)	Yes, but with some mistakes (1 point)	Yes, did this very well (2 points)
ask what the problem is?			
ask for details?			
diagnose the problem?			
give advice?			
confirm a solution?			

Result _____ / 10 marks

Cut along this line

Working with words

Complete these sentences with verbs from the list. Change the form of the verb if necessary.

pick   take   feed   put   make

1 We _____ all our furniture out of real wood.

2 _____ the boxes up and put them on the lorry.

3 Sorry! I _____ the paper into the fax machine really slowly, but it's jammed.

4 The nuts are _____ out of their shells using this machine.

5 Can you _____ about ten litres of petrol into the engine?

Match 6–11 to a–f.

6 You're ready to go, … ___

7 The basic procedure is … ___

8 Essentially, there are three … ___

9 First … ___

10 Having finished that, … ___

11 Finally, you're … ___

a of all, press this.

b ready to go.

c quite simple.

d once you've switched it on.

e it's ready to eat.

f main stages.

Business communication skills

Complete this conversation with the missing words.

A Hello. Can you [12]s _____ a couple of [13]m _____?

B Yes, what can I [14]d _____ for you?

A That was a very interesting talk. I'd like to know some more about the process and I was [15]w_____ if you'd [16]l _____ to join me for a drink.

B That would be [17]n _____, but I'm a bit [18]t _____ up at the moment.

A It can't be [19]h _____. Well, I'd be [20]d _____ if you would join me later – perhaps for dinner?

B That would be [21]g _____.

Language at work

Complete these sentences with the active or passive form of the verbs in brackets.

22 Try to _____ (notice) by your boss as quickly as possible if you want a promotion.

23 People prefer to _____ (do) business with people they like.

24 Staff must _____ (warn) if they break any rules.

25 I _____ (give) this report by your secretary a few minutes ago.

26 If you _____ (invite) to dinner in Germany it's a good idea to be on time.

27 Jatropha plants can _____ (plant) on infertile ground.

28 The conveyor belt _____ (carry) the components to this box here.

29 My company _____ (found) in 1958 by two brothers.

30 We can _____ (fire) you if you turn up late for work.

Result _____ / 30 marks

Role cards

Copy this page and cut out the role cards for the students. Students should do both role-plays. Then use the *Speaking test results* forms to evaluate each student's performance. You can then cut out the results and give them to the students.

Cut along this line

Student A

1 You work in IT and you are very busy, but your colleague needs help. Answer the phone and respond:

- explain that the procedure is simple and follows this sequence: click on the old anti-virus icon; click on 'renew'; you are directed to the website; follow the instructions and put in credit card details; the software is automatically downloaded
- respond to your colleague's invitation.

2 You meet your colleague in the corridor. Get his / her attention. You need some help:

- tell your colleague that you need a new assistant in your department
- ask for an explanation of how the recruitment procedure works
- thank your colleague for his / her help and invite him / her to your office after the meeting to discuss the job requirements in detail.

Student B

1 You know your colleague in IT is busy, but you need to call him / her. Call and do the following:

- ask if your colleague has time to talk
- ask for an explanation of how to renew the anti-virus software on the computer
- thank your colleague for his / her help and invite him / her for a drink after work.

2 You are head of recruitment at a company. You are late for a meeting, but a colleague stops you in the corridor. Say you are busy, but agree to help:

- explain that the procedure is simple and follows this sequence: details of the job are given to you; a job advert is put in the trade press or newspaper; you make a shortlist of applicants; they are interviewed by you and your colleague
- respond to your colleague's invitation.

Cut along this line

Speaking test results

Use these forms to evaluate the students.

Cut along this line

Student A

Can the student …	Didn't do this (0 points)	Yes, but with some mistakes (1 point)	Yes, did this very well (2 points)
respond to a request for help?			
describe the basic procedure?			
explain stages?			
use expressions to show sequence?			
accept or decline an invitation?			

Result _____ / 10 marks

Student B

Can the student …	Didn't do this (0 points)	Yes, but with some mistakes (1 point)	Yes, did this very well (2 points)
respond to a request for help?			
describe the basic procedure?			
explain stages?			
use expressions to show sequence?			
accept or decline an invitation?			

Result _____ / 10 marks

Cut along this line

Working with words

Choose the correct answer from the words in *italics*.

1 What we look for in staff is 100% *dedication / punctuality* to the job.

2 Most importantly, nurses must be very *confident / caring* people.

3 The most highly *motivated / patient* staff are not those who want a bonus, but those who naturally want to make things work.

4 We don't really work fixed hours. Some days you might work late and other days you might leave a little earlier. We like a *flexible / helpful* approach to the working day.

5 I'm afraid your work record so far hasn't been very good. You don't seem very *dependable / dependant*. For example, last month you were late for work four times.

6 I remember when I was as *creative / ambitious* as him and wanted to reach the top of the company.

7 *Patience / Enthusiasm* is a key quality in customer care, especially when you have to listen to customers complaining about products.

8 One of the *most creative / hardest-working* members of staff is Gill. She's always here first. I think we should give her a bonus.

Business communication skills

There is one mistake in each phrase. Correct it.

9 We're very please with your performance.

10 You done a good job.

11 You seem to be do very well.

12 Perhaps one thing to work along is your communication skills.

13 How do you think about these changes?

14 How are you getting up with your new job?

15 One of your key strongs is listening.

16 I think this is an area for improve.

17 So let summarize what we've agreed.

18 One thing you're going do is a training course.

19 How does that hear to you?

20 Are there anything else you'd like to add?

Language at work

Complete these sentences with the past perfect or past continuous of the verbs in brackets.

21 I _____ (work) in a hotel bar when I first met him.

22 I mentioned it, and he said he _____ (already / ask) them.

23 By the time they arrived, the guests _____ (leave) and gone home.

24 Why _____ (you / talk) to them just now? You're not thinking of working for them, are you?

25 She ate her sandwich while she _____ (still / work) on her computer. It isn't good for her.

26 The appraisal said he _____ (not / improve) his performance in the last six months and things needed to change.

27 When I first started in business, they _____ (not / invent) computers!

28 I don't think he _____ (do) anything when I spoke to him earlier, so he probably has time to help.

29 Can I have a word? Why _____ (you / send) an email to a friend when I walked past your desk just now? You know our rules on that, don't you?

30 I saw the report on the accident, but only after the same thing _____ (happen) three more times.

Result _____ / 30 marks

Speaking test

Role cards

Copy this page and cut out the role cards for the students. Students should do both role-plays. Then use the *Speaking test results* forms to evaluate each student's performance. You can then cut out the results and give them to the students.

Cut along this line

Student A

1 You are giving a six-month performance review to an employee in your sales office:

- tell the employee that you're very happy with his / her performance
- comment on his / her teamwork
- find out how he / she feels
- suggest that he / she takes some training in sales on the telephone
- summarize the discussion and set some objectives.

2 You are having your six-month performance review with the manager of your sales office:

- explain that you are not very happy because you don't think you are being given enough responsibility
- say you would like more involvement in the recruitment process of new staff.
- request training in report-writing.

Student B

1 You are having your six-month performance review with the manager of your sales office:

- explain that you are basically happy, but that you would like to make more sales
- request some computer training with Excel.

2 You are giving a six-month performance review to an employee in your human resources department:

- tell the employee that you're fairly happy with his / her performance
- comment on the good work he / she has done so far
- find out how he / she feels
- suggest that he / she takes some training in how to interview candidates for jobs
- summarize the discussion and set some objectives.

Cut along this line

Speaking test results

Use these forms to evaluate the students.

Cut along this line

Student A

Can the student ...	Didn't do this (0 points)	Yes, but with some mistakes (1 point)	Yes, did this very well (2 points)
assess overall performance?			
give feedback?			
encourage self-evaluation?			
suggest some objectives?			
set and agree some objectives?			

Result _____ / 10 marks

Student B

Can the student ...	Didn't do this (0 points)	Yes, but with some mistakes (1 point)	Yes, did this very well (2 points)
assess overall performance?			
give feedback?			
encourage self-evaluation?			
suggest some objectives?			
set and agree some objectives?			

Result _____ / 10 marks

Cut along this line

Working with words

Complete these sentences with the missing prepositions.

1 They managed _____ take the silk into Europe.

2 We succeeded _____ winning the contract.

3 Can you find _____ how our partner in Vietnam is doing?

4 I've been looking _____ your proposal. It looks good.

5 How did you come _____ that piece of information?

Choose the correct answer from the words in *italics*.

6 The meeting was a *complete / significant* disaster. Nothing went right.

7 Don't you think that all those hours spent in meetings are a total *waste of time / flop*?

8 Your speech was a real *triumph / know-how*. What a success!

9 His most *amazing / complete* achievement has been to work for the same company for over forty years!

10 I think we need to bring in some outside *breakthrough / expertise* to help us finish this.

Business communication skills

Complete this conversation with verbs from the list. Change the form of the verb if necessary.

underline   say   focus   tell   be   give   learn

A How ¹¹_____ your trip?

B Very interesting.

A So, ¹²_____ me an overview.

B Well, I was really impressed. The factory is clean and well-organized. We could ¹³_____ a lot from them.

A Why do you ¹⁴_____ that?

B They work in small groups, rather than in lines. It seems more efficient and improves quality. It ¹⁵_____ the importance of sharing know-how.

A That's interesting. Maybe we should ¹⁶_____ on running some kind of exchange between staff. So, ¹⁷_____ me more.

Complete this conversation with verbs from the list. Change the form of the verb if necessary.

go (x2)   be (x2)   make   concentrate   expect   fill

A How did it ¹⁸_____ at the conference? What ¹⁹_____ your overall impressions?

B Well, there ²⁰_____ no big surprises.

A Did you see Mr Chau?

B Oh yes. Let me ²¹_____ you in on what he's doing. Actually our meeting couldn't have ²²_____ better. What he's proposing is some kind of merger.

A Rather like what we were thinking.

B Yes, but this wouldn't be a joint venture. It would be a merger of both companies.

A That isn't really what I ²³_____.

B What ²⁴_____ you say that?

A We don't really want a full merger. Maybe we need to ²⁵_____ on our proposal for a joint venture.

Language at work

Combine and transform the two sentences with the contrasting word in brackets. See the example.

(despite + ing) She still hasn't called that client. I asked her to call him four times.

Despite asking her to call him four times, she still hasn't called that client.

26 (although) I'm busy. I can help you for an hour.

_____

27 (despite + ing) She was late this morning. She was warned yesterday about it.

_____

28 (even though) I told her you were busy. She demanded to speak to you.

_____

29 (however) Things look bad. We must keep trying.

_____

30 (despite + noun) The last plan didn't work. Let's try again.

_____

Result _____ / 30 marks

Role cards

Copy this page and cut out the role cards for the students. Students should do both role-plays. Then use the *Speaking test results* forms to evaluate each student's performance. You can then cut out the results and give them to the students.

Cut along this line

Student A

1 Your company sells clothes. You have just been on a trip to Thailand to look at a factory. Give your colleague the following feedback:

• the trip was useful
• the factory is efficient and modern, and staff seem very motivated
• they would like to supply us.

Suggest next step – to invite their CEO to your country.

2 Your company runs communication skills training. Your colleague has just been to visit potential clients in Paris.

Ask for feedback on the trip.

Student B

1 Your company sells clothes. Your colleague has just been to Thailand.

Ask for feedback on the trip.

2 Your company runs communication skills training. You have just been to visit potential clients in Paris. Give your colleague the following feedback:

• the trip was interesting, but no firm agreements
• the companies already have training from French companies, but they were interested in receiving training in English and maybe English lessons
• two companies were very interested and want prices.

Suggest next step – to send information and make follow-up calls next week.

Cut along this line

Speaking test results

Use these forms to evaluate the students.

Cut along this line

Student A

Can the student ...	Didn't do this (0 points)	Yes, but with some mistakes (1 point)	Yes, did this very well (2 points)
say how the trip went?			
give a general evaluation?			
report back on what happened?			
report final outcome of the trip?			
suggest the next step?			

Result _____ / 10 marks

Student B

Can the student ...	Didn't do this (0 points)	Yes, but with some mistakes (1 point)	Yes, did this very well (2 points)
say how the trip went?			
give a general evaluation?			
report back on what happened?			
report final outcome of the trip?			
suggest the next step?			

Result _____ / 10 marks

Cut along this line

Unit 1

1 routine + fun
2 rewarding + good
3 demanding + glamorous
4 varied + dull
5 stressful + depressing
6 challenging + worthwhile
7 c
8 f
9 d
10 e
11 b
12 g
13 a
14 oversee
15 deal
16 handle
17 tell
18 sounds
19 responsible
20 charge
21 involve
22 Do you work in Quebec?
23 Can I ask who your main supplier is?
24 Which parts of the world does your company supply?
25 Do you know where Lisa works?
26 How many hours a week do you work?
27 The phone rings all the time.
28 We hardly ever leave the office before seven.
29 I'd say I play tennis about three times a week.
30 There's normally a staff meeting on Mondays. / Normally, there's a staff meeting on Mondays.

Unit 2

1 deadline
2 schedule
3 track
4 resources
5 budget
6 tasks
7 updates
8 objectives
9 skills
10 job
11 How
12 What
13 where
14 Can / Could
15 Why
16 14
17 15
18 13
19 11
20 12
21 is
22 with
23 to
24 your
25 is taking
26 need
27 'm emailing
28 understand
29 think
30 're interviewing

Unit 3

1 exciting
2 boring
3 relaxing
4 exhilarating
5 interesting
6 frightened
7 enjoyable
8 tiring
9 How do you find our country?
10 How often do they visit head office?
11 What sort of films do you like?
12 in
13 of
14 on
15 about
16 about
17 on
18 back
19–21 Michela called. Call her back on 007 393 110294 or email her at michela-13@enterprise_1.fi
22 have you met
23 came
24 was

25 've never been
26 Have you ever been
27 did you go
28 went
29 was
30 've put

Unit 4

1 user-friendly
2 up-to-date
3 immediate
4 convenient
5 accurate
6 efficient
7 personal
8 time-saving
9 e
10 a
11 c
12 b
13 d
14 at
15 in
16 in
17 of
18 on
19 On
20 more stressful
21 fast
22 friendly
23 more complicated
24 longer
25 more convenient
26 slightly
27 isn't nearly
28 the better
29 great
30 little

Unit 5

1 guarantee
2 service
3 monitor
4 satisfaction
5 requirements
6 expectations
7 assistant
8 care
9 provide

10 in
11 little / bit
12 with
13 about
14 possible / OK
15 How / What
16 suits
17 make
18 bring
19 prefer
20 fine / OK / perfect / good
21–25 (2 marks per sentence. Take 0.5 off per error. Note that some variation in answers may be possible.)
21 I am writing to confirm our meeting on Friday the 4th.
22 We are meeting at 10 a.m. in my office.
23 The bus to our company leaves from the train station every fifteen minutes.
24 Please note that our head of sales is also joining us.
25 I look forward to seeing you.

Unit 6

1 trip
2 journey
3 travel
4 check
5 facilities
6 speciality
7 entertainment
8 excursion
9 sightseeing
10 hospitality
11 nightlife
12 up
13 up
14 around
15 in
16 up
17 out
18 a
19 h
20 f
21 e
22 b
23 g

24 d
25 have to
26 need
27 supposed
28 mustn't
29 allowed
30 don't need

Unit 7

1 safety
2 security
3 password
4 breach
5 access
6 pass
7 prevent
8 safeguard
9 monitor
10 c
11 f
12 a
13 h
14 b
15 g
16 d
17 i
18 e
19 Have you heard
20 has happened
21 has resigned
22 has been stealing
23 has been doing
24 have never seen
25 haven't they fired
26 have been talking
27 Consequently
28 So that
29 so
30 because of

Unit 8

1 responsibility
2 complementary
3 forces
4 alliance
5 player
6 ground
7 closely
8 venture

9 next step
10 intend to
11 likely that
12 timescale on
13 the deadline
14 going to
15 planned to
16 Well done
17 chances are
18 I expect
19 In
20 by
21 Over / In
22 by
23 in
24 on
25 should
26 will
27 're going to
28 might
29 'll
30 should

Unit 9

1 components
2 inventory
3 supplier
4 distributed
5 raw
6 out
7 low
8 out
9 of
10 on
11 in
12 following
13 find
14 take
15 place
16 according
17 put
18 asap
19 problem
20 look
21 to
22 out
23 on
24 about
25 of
26 to

27 he had / has looked into
28 told him
29 had sent / sent
30 asked you to call

Unit 10

1 cramped
2 up-to-date
3 run down
4 well equipped
5 c
6 c
7 b
8 c
9 How / What
10 Why
11 Have
12 Could / Can
13 Maybe
14 prove
15 consider
16 better
17 worth
18 reservations
19 rather
20 work
21 sure
22 c
23 e
24 f
25 h
26 d
27 i
28 a
29 b
30 g

Unit 11

1 have
2 make
3 go
4 carry
5 reached
6 put
7 make
8 have
9 avoid
10 express
11 backing

12 favour
13 majority
14 brainstorm
15 compromise
16 From my ~~opinion~~ of view it's a bad idea. (point)
17 As ~~near~~ as I'm concerned, it's fine. (far)
18 I'm not quite sure ~~for~~ that. (about)
19 I ~~listen~~ what you're saying, but it won't work. (hear)
20 You're absolutely right. I couldn't agree ~~much~~. (more)
21 To be ~~truth~~ I don't see how we're going to persuade them. (honest)
22 I ~~have~~ your point about the costs, but I think it's worth it. (take / see)
23 Let's ~~see~~ it, he's too old for the job! (face)
24 could
25 will
26 will
27 needed
28 would
29 would
30 will

Unit 12

1 original
2 up
3 prototype
4 obstacles
5 sophisticated
6 traditional
7 concept
8 dynamic
9 a
10 g
11 b
12 c
13 e
14 f
15 d
16 d
17 f
18 e
19 a
20 c
21 b

22 worst
23 most expensive
24 friendliest / most friendly
25 most valuable
26 highest
27 lowest
28 latest
29 most well known / best known
30 happiest

Unit 13

1 fault
2 flaw
3 misunderstanding
4 down
5 incompatible
6 has broken down
7 unreliable
8 out of order
9 failure
10 failures
11 matter
12 keeps
13 mean
14 tried
15 trouble
16 always
17 might
18 best
19 help
20 exactly
21 sort
22 like
23 ✗ I think you should ask for help.
24 ✓
25 ✗ I'd speak to her if I were / was you.
26 ✓
27 ✗ Is it easy enough for you?
28 ✓
29 ✓
30 ✗ The main problem is that we don't have enough resources.

Unit 14

1 make
2 Pick
3 fed
4 taken

5 put
6 d
7 c
8 f
9 a
10 e
11 b
12 spare
13 minutes
14 do
15 wondering
16 like
17 nice
18 tied
19 helped
20 delighted
21 good / great
22 be noticed
23 do
24 be warned
25 was given
26 are invited
27 be planted
28 carries
29 was founded
30 fire

Unit 15

1 dedication
2 caring
3 motivated
4 flexible
5 dependable
6 ambitious
7 Patience
8 hardest-working
9 We're very pleased with your performance.
10 You've done a good job.
11 You seem to be doing very well.
12 Perhaps one thing to work on is your communication skills.
13 What do you think about these changes? / How do you feel about these changes?
14 How are you getting on with your new job?
15 One of your key strengths is listening.
16 I think this is an area for

improvement.
17 So let's summarize what we've agreed.
18 One thing you're going to do is a training course.
19 How does that sound to you?
20 Is there anything else you'd like to add?
21 was working
22 'd / had already asked
23 had left
24 were you talking
25 was still working
26 hadn't improved
27 hadn't invented
28 was doing
29 were you sending
30 had happened

Unit 16

1 to
2 in
3 out
4 at
5 across
6 complete
7 waste of time
8 triumph
9 amazing
10 expertise
11 was
12 give
13 learn
14 say
15 underlines
16 focus
17 tell
18 go
19 were
20 were
21 fill
22 gone
23 expected
24 makes
25 concentrate
26 Although I'm busy, I can help you for an hour.
27 She was late this morning despite being warned yesterday about it.

28 Even though I told her you were busy, she demanded to speak to you. / She demanded to speak to you, even though I told her you were busy.
29 Things look bad. However, we must keep trying.
30 Despite the last plan not working, let's try again. / Let's try again, despite the last plan not working.

Unit 1

Working with words

2 glamorous
3 demanding
4 challenging
5 routine
6 dull, depressing
7 stressful
8 fun
9 worthwhile, rewarding

Business communication skills

Exercise 1

2 this is   3 Nice to meet you
4 I'm pleased to   5 So tell me
6 in charge of   7 sounds
8 deal with

Exercise 2

2 I'm delighted to meet you
3 We're responsible for
4 It involves a lot of testing
5 I'd like to introduce you to

Language at work

Exercise 1

2 spends
3 misses
4 tries
5 you find
6 does your job involve
7 Do you work
8 don't
9 Are you
10 am

Exercise 2

2 I often have lunch in the staff restaurant.
3 I occasionally have lunch with clients.
4 I usually finish work at 4.00 p.m. on Friday afternoons.
5 I hardly ever work on Saturdays.
6 I never work on Sundays – this is a personal rule of mine.

Unit 2

Working with words

Exercise 1

2 schedule   3 update   4 budget
5 deadline   6 teamwork   7 skills

Exercise 2

2 d   3 f   4 b   5 g
6 h   7 c   8 e

Exercise 3

1 deadline   2 schedule   3 allocated
4 resources   5 staff   6 budget
7 update

Business communication skills

Exercise 1

2 h   3 d   4 k   5 m   6 j
7 a   8 i   9 n   10 l   11 c
12 e   13 b   14 f

Exercise 2

2 So far so good
3 everything is going according to plan
4 everything is on track
5 need somebody to
6 why don't I

Language at work

Exercise 1

2 do you have to
3 is she sitting
4 are you working on
5 does Nadia think
6 Are you thinking
7 does a successful salesperson earn
8 are you doing
9 think / belongs
10 are having

Exercise 2

2 f   3 g   4 a   5 h
6 d   7 b   8 e

Unit 3

Working with words

Exercise 1

2 make   3 work   4 do
5 work   6 Do   7 make
8 take

Exercise 2

2 boring   3 relaxed
4 exhilarating 5 tiring
6 interested   7 exciting
8 tired

Business communication skills

Exercise 1

2 b   3 c   4 c   5 b   6 a
7 a   8 c   9 b   10 a

Exercise 2

2 00 44 319 44 010
3 Lydia_49@yahoo.dt
4 www.about-me.com/courses_online

Language at work

Exercise 1

2 closed   3 has / organized
4 Have / called   5 did / arrive
6 have / met   7 didn't take
8 haven't improved 9 Have / spoken
10 have / worked

Exercise 2

2 since   3 for   4 for   5 since

Unit 4

Working with words

Exercise 1

2 cost-effective   3 convenient
4 secure   5 time-saving
6 efficient   7 easier
8 user-friendly   9 up-to-date
10 accurate   11 immediate

Exercise 2

2 financial adviser   3 online banking
4 business class

Business communication skills

Exercise 1

2 Let me explain how it works
3 The main thing to note is
4 What happens is
5 One other useful feature is that
6 What happens when
7 You can see what happens when you

Exercise 2

2 similar / different
3 benefit / drawback
4 As well as / also
5 downside / plus side
6 Whereas before / now
7 one / other
8 difficult / simple
9 more / better

Language at work

Exercise 1

2 easy   3 well
4 friendlier   5 faster
6 slower   7 more original
8 more popular

Exercise 2

2 than   3 than   4 slightly
5 far   6 much   7 a bit
8 as   9 as

Unit 5

Working with words

Exercise 1

2 requirements   3 service
4 care   5 expectations
6 satisfaction

Exercise 2

2 tailor   3 guarantee   4 evaluate
5 ensure   6 adjust   7 provide

Exercise 3

1 services   2 guarantee   3 evaluate
4 adapt   5 care   6 satisfy

Business communication skills

Exercise 1
2 arrange 3 make 4 good
5 How 6 suit 7 'd prefer

Exercise 2
2 in 3 with 4 for
5 for 6 on 7 back
8 forward

Exercise 3
1 c 2 a 3 f 4 d
5 e 6 h 7 b 8 g

Language at work

Exercise 1
2 gets in
3 is meeting
4 is bringing
5 are we all having lunch
6 are showing
7 are we doing
8 are having
9 does your flight leave
10 leaves

Exercise 2
2 Our team is going out to celebrate Torsten's birthday.
3 We're meeting in reception at 5.30 p.m.
4 Then we're having a meal in that new Greek restaurant.
5 The last train leaves at midnight.

Unit 6

Working with words

Exercise 1
2 exhibition 3 excursion
4 entertainment 5 sightseeing
6 specialities 7 venue
European city = Alicante

Exercise 2
2 check in 3 freshen up
4 show you around 5 eat out
6 go out 7 pick you up
8 meet up with

Business communication skills

Exercise 1
2 It's nice to finally meet you
3 Likewise
4 how was your journey
5 did you have any trouble
6 let me take your bag
7 can I get you a drink
8 sounds great
9 let me run through
10 get a chance

Exercise 2
2 to 3 to 4 with
5 opportunity 6 over 7 over
8 own 9 remind 10 wish

Language at work

Exercise 1
2 need to / have to bring your laptop – we have one you can use
3 allowed to smoke in this area
4 mustn't take these documents out of the building
5 supposed to talk in the library

Exercise 2
2 be polite and helpful to customers
   wear an ID badge at all times
3 leave bicycles at the back of the shop
   enter the shop through the main entrance
4 smoke in the warehouse
   wear jeans

Unit 7

Working with words

Exercise 1
2 for 3 from 4 against
5 against 6 for

Exercise 2
2 identity theft
3 unauthorized access
4 PIN number
5 X-ray machine
6 security breach
7 CCTV
8 antivirus software

Business communication skills

Exercise 1
2 As it stands, the situation is
3 This is because of the fact that
4 As a result
5 I'd like to update you
6 By entering
7 We expect

Exercise 2
2 I don't quite understand how it works.
3 Can you tell us more about it?
4 What do you mean by 'security breach'?
5 If I understand you correctly, this will cost a lot.
6 I'm not sure I follow you.

Language at work

Exercise 1
2 has been ringing
3 haven't / switched
4 have been looking
5 have just called
6 have sent
7 Have / had
8 have been talking

Exercise 2
2 so
3 In order to
4 so that
5 Therefore

Unit 8

Working with words

Exercise 1
2 c 3 g 4 f 5 h 6 j
7 b 8 d 9 e 10 a

Exercise 2
2 take responsibility
3 team player
4 work closely
5 complementary skills
6 common ground
7 form alliances
8 joint venture
9 mutual benefit
10 shared goal

Business communication skills

Exercise 1
2 What's the timescale on this
3 we plan to
4 in the long run

Exercise 2
2 hope to have
3 in the short term
4 in the long term
5 How long will it take to
6 expect
7 by the end of
8 going to tell everyone
9 this leave us
10 over the next
11 chances are

Language at work

Exercise 1
2 'm / am going to 3 'll / will
4 'll / will 5 'm / am going to
6 'll / will

Exercise 2
2 c 3 c 4 a 5 b 6 a

Unit 9

Working with words

Exercise 1
2 supplier 3 distributors
4 inventory 5 streamline
6 chain 7 Logistics
8 client 9 warehouse
10 component 11 raw
12 retailer

Exercise 2

2 stock up on   3 out of
4 track of   5 running low

Business communication skills

Exercise 1

2 Can I take your account details
3 look into it
4 according to my information
5 what has happened to it
6 you check it out for me
7 get back to you within the hour

Exercise 2

2 it was dispatched on
3 something must have gone wrong
4 check it out
5 asap
6 as quick as we can
7 charge it to

Language at work

Exercise 1

2 would deal with it straight away
3 had happened to it
4 was off sick
5 would look into it
6 if she was better
7 hadn't been off sick
8 had said
9 me he had sent the order

Exercise 2

2 Bella asked Alan if he wanted anything from the canteen.
3 Nabila wants to know what the time of the next flight to Boston is.
4 Richard asked Sally if / whether she wanted to borrow *The Economist*.
5 Keith says he's tired of dealing with unreliable suppliers.
6 Jackie told me that if I couldn't go to the meeting, she would go instead.

Unit 10

Working with words

Exercise 1

2 badly equipped   3 state-of-the-art
4 spacious   5 well maintained
6 well equipped   7 run down
8 old-fashioned

Exercise 2

2 quite   3 really   4 quite
5 fairly   6 pretty   7 extremely
8 very

Business communication skills

Exercise 1

2 change the colour
3 asking them to make a better offer

4 difficult to convince them about our proposals
5 we provide some chairs
6 having music in the factory
7 not come (if you don't mind)
8 we look at this again tomorrow morning

Exercise 2

2 good idea   3 would work
4 on top   5 in addition
6 Besides

Language at work

Exercise 1

2 ✓   3 ✓
4 X little few   5 X many much
6 ✓   7 X any some
8 X fewer less   9 ✓
10 ✓

Exercise 2

2 few   3 many / any
4 some / a lot   5 much
6 lot   7 many / any
8 any   9 lot of / few

Unit 11

Working with words

Exercise 1

2 brainstorming   3 put forward
4 majority   5 backing
6 carry out

Exercise 2

2 a   3 g   4 e   5 h
6 c   7 d   8 b

Exercise 3

2 consensus   3 options
4 evaluate   5 confrontation
6 compromise

Business communication skills

Exercise 1

2 agree   3 face   4 point
5 thing   6 As   7 Absolutely
8 Come   9 correctly   10 agreed

Exercise 2

2 not quiet sure not quite sure
3 I am hearing what you say I hear what you are saying
4 enough fair fair enough
5 As far I'm concerned As far as I'm concerned
6 fine to me fine with me

Language at work

Exercise 1

2 have / will end
3 work / you will be
4 knew / would be
5 had / would they be

6 improves / will have to
7 would you feel / asked you
8 would do / went
9 could / would you do
10 arrive / will be able to

Exercise 2

2 could   3 Unless / I'll have
4 Unless / will look   5 will have to / if

Unit 12

Working with words

Exercise 1

2 a   3 a   4 a   5 b
6 c   7 c   8 b   9 a

Exercise 2

2 prototype   3 concept
4 reliable   5 simple
6 innovative   7 revolutionary

Business communication skills

Exercise 1

2 about   3 by   4 at
5 at   6 for   7 about
8 to   9 on   10 with

Exercise 2

1 Good   2 here   3 start / begin
4 First   5 Then   6 finally
7 free

Exercise 3

2 d   3 k   4 a   5 e   6 g   7 b
8 l   9 i   10 f   11 c   12 j

Language at work

Exercise 1

2 I think quickest I think the quickest
3 the more the most
4 we ever we have ever
5 boredest most bored
6 a second the second
7 you ever you have ever
8 the most busiest the busiest

Exercise 2

2 worst   3 fewest   4 flexible
5 second   6 has   7 fewest
8 best

Unit 13

Working with words

Exercise 1

2 failure   3 faulty
4 breakdowns   5 unreliable
6 damaged   7 defective

Exercise 2

2 c   3 c   4 a   5 c   6 b   7 a

Business communication skills

Exercise 1
2 won't
3 do you mean by
4 keeps on
5 sounds as though
6 Have you tried
7 advise you to
8 should solve the problem
9 if I were you

Exercise 2
2 's always borrowing
3 taking
4 wrong
5 should
6 advise
7 sounds
8 solve
9 appears
10 putting

Language at work

Exercise 1
2 have to   3 shouldn't   4 should
5 could   6 should   7 should
8 would

Exercise 2
2 b 3 f 4 a 5 c 6 g 7 d 8 h

Exercise 3
2 ~~very tired~~ too tired
3 ~~responses enough~~ enough responses
4 ~~not enough clearly~~ not clearly enough
5 ~~too much expensive~~ too expensive / much too expensive
6 ~~I have time enough~~ I don't have enough time

Unit 14

Working with words

Exercise 1
2 with   3 up   4 in
5 into   6 stages 7 end

Exercise 2
2 e 3 a 4 f 5 d 6 c

Exercise 3
2 essentially   3 there are
4 First of all   5 Having
6 Once you've done 7 you're ready to

Business communication skills

Exercise 1
2 we'd be delighted   3 I was wondering if
4 how about

Exercise 2
2 I'm afraid something has come up.
3 That would be great.
4 I'm sorry for messing you around, but how about the week after?

Exercise 3
2 c 3 a 4 e 5 b 6 j
7 i 8 f 9 d 10 g

Language at work

Exercise 1
2 make
3 starts / are cut and painted
4 sew
5 are washed
6 employs
7 supports
8 are encouraged and trained

Exercise 2
2 is located   3 was chosen
4 was needed   5 was held
6 was won

Exercise 3
2 was set up twenty years ago (by Hans Angst)
3 must be sacked (by the manager) for being late
4 have agreed to extend the hours of work
5 is regarded as a sign of politeness in this culture

Unit 15

Working with words

Exercise 1
2 confident   3 ambitious
4 patient   5 hard-working
6 enthusiastic 7 punctual

Exercise 2
2 –ability   3 –ing   4 –ion
5 –ful   6 –le   7 –m

Business communication skills

Exercise 1
2 pleased / happy   3 feel
4 happy   5 strengths
6 seem   7 thing

Exercise 2
2 about   3 for   4 with

Exercise 3
2 do   3 intend 4 sound
5 add

Language at work

Exercise 1
2 hadn't been   3 were all finishing
4 said   5 hadn't asked
6 was suggesting   7 stopped
8 came   9 hadn't liked
10 had waited

Exercise 2
2 had had   3 were / becoming
4 was growing   5 had / graduated
6 were running   7 had asked
8 hadn't / taken   9 was doing

Unit 16

Working with words

Exercise 1
2 c 3 a 4 a 5 a 6 a

Exercise 2
2 complete waste of time
3 significant breakthrough
4 great success
5 amazing achievement

Business communication skills

Exercise 1
2 i 3 h 4 a 5 e 6 j
7 b 8 g 9 f 10 c

Exercise 2
2 I'll fill you in
3 So, give me an overview
4 this underlines the importance of
5 could have gone better
6 how did it go?
7 what we need to do is
8 Tell me more
9 We should focus on

Language at work

Exercise 1
2 Even though she is bad at paperwork, she is our best salesperson / Even though she is our best salesperson, she is bad at paperwork.
3 Despite only having two products, it is an extremely successful business.
4 They went ahead with the project, despite the fact that the research was unfavourable.
5 Although the meeting went on and on, we made some useful decisions.
6 He didn't know that the company was for sale. However, he did have an idea of how much it was worth.

Exercise 2
2 The seminar was a waste of time. However, we enjoyed meeting our new colleagues. / We enjoyed meeting our new colleagues. However, the seminar was a waste of time.
3 He was miserable, but he earned a lot of money.
4 Despite the fact that we forgot our notes, we managed to give the presentation. / Despite forgetting our notes, we managed to give the presentation.
5 The office was big, but there wasn't enough space for all the desks.

Needs analysis form

Section 1

Name _____

_____

Company / organization details _____

_____

_____

Job title / description _____

_____

_____

Have you studied English before? Yes / No

If you answered 'yes', give details (where / when?).

_____

_____

_____

What did you like / dislike about your previous English

lessons? _____

_____

_____

Teacher's notes / comments

_____

_____

_____

_____

_____

_____

_____

_____

_____

_____

_____

_____

_____

Section 2

**Read the sentences and tick the correct answer for you.
Please give more details where possible.**

For my job, I mainly communicate …
   with clients in other companies. ☐
   with colleagues inside the company. ☐
   with clients and colleagues. ☐

Details _____

_____

_____

I mainly communicate in English with …
   non-native speakers. ☐
   native speakers. ☐
   both native and non-native speakers. ☐

When I communicate in English …
   I need to be fluent and it's not a problem if I
   make a few mistakes. ☐
   I shouldn't make any mistakes with grammar,
   pronunciation, or vocabulary. ☐

Details _____

_____

_____

When I use English at work …
   speaking is the most important form of communication. ☐
   writing is the most important form of communication. ☐
   speaking and writing are equally important. ☐

Details _____

_____

_____

For my job …
   I need to learn specialist English. ☐
   I need to learn general English. ☐
   I need to learn specialist and general English. ☐

Details _____

_____

_____

Section 3

To respond in this section, circle a number.
1 = It isn't very important for me.
2 = It isn't important for my job, but it could be interesting.
3 = It's sometimes important and it could be useful to practise.
4 = It's very important for me and we must practise this language in my classes.

How important is it for you to be able to …
introduce yourself and describe what you do at work?	1	2	3	4
discuss projects you are working on?	1	2	3	4
talk about free time and hobbies?	1	2	3	4
explain how something works?	1	2	3	4
deal with customers?	1	2	3	4
welcome visitors?	1	2	3	4
explain changes?	1	2	3	4
present and discuss plans?	1	2	3	4
deal with orders?	1	2	3	4
discuss your place of work?	1	2	3	4
discuss and make decisions?	1	2	3	4
give presentations?	1	2	3	4
solve problems?	1	2	3	4
describe processes and make appointments?	1	2	3	4
give feedback and set objectives?	1	2	3	4
give reports?	1	2	3	4

How important are these communication skills for you?
Social / Conversational English	1	2	3	4
Making telephone calls	1	2	3	4
Attending meetings	1	2	3	4
Giving and attending presentations	1	2	3	4
Writing emails	1	2	3	4

Do you speak and listen in other situations? Please give details.

_____

_____

_____

Do you read or write other correspondence?

Please give details.

_____

_____

_____

Section 4

1 How much time do you have for self-study on this course?

_____ hours per week.

2 Write two questions you have about this course for your teacher.

For example: *Will we have time to study financial vocabulary …?*

Question 1

_____

_____

_____

_____

_____

Question 2

_____

_____

_____

_____

_____

Your teacher will return this form to you and answer your questions below.

Answer to question 1 _____

_____

_____

_____

Answer to question 2 _____

_____

_____

_____

Materials used in the lesson

- *Business Result Placement test*, available at www.oup.com/elt/teacher/result
- *Needs analysis form* (photocopied from pages 126 and 127 of the Teacher's Book)
- *Contents* page of *Business Result Intermediate Student's Book*

Part 1 | How do you find out the needs of students?

1 Imagine you have a new student and that you have access to the following sources of information. What kind of information could you find out from each one?

- the student's training manager

_____

- the website for the student's company

_____

- the student's line manager

_____

- the results from the placement test

_____

- the student's job description

_____

- a report from the student's previous English course tutor

_____

- copies of correspondence received in the student's department

_____

- the names of other companies that the student does business with

_____

2 ▶ Watch this section and answer questions 1–3.

1 What kind of needs analysis does John (the co-author) think most teachers should carry out? Is this true for you or your school?

_____

_____

2 What kind of information do we find out about Andreas (the student) in this first part of the needs analysis?

_____

_____

3 What are Andreas's views on the best way to learn English? Do you agree with him? Do your students have similar views?

_____

_____

Part 2 | What kind of information do you need to find out?

3 ▶ Watch this section and answer questions 1–2.

1 What does John suggest a needs analysis must find out? List the three types of question a teacher can ask.

_____

_____

_____

2 As Cathy (the teacher) interviews Andreas, complete Section 2 on a photocopy of the *Needs analysis* form (pages 126–127).

4 ▶ The needs analysis interview is the teacher's first chance to evaluate a student's spoken English. Watch the previous sections from the DVD again and make notes about Andreas's strengths and weaknesses, including any specific errors.

Strengths	Weaknesses

5 Which areas of Andreas's English would you give immediate attention to?

_____

_____

Part 3 | How do you analyse the information?

6 After the interview, the teacher asked Andreas to complete the rest of the form. Read the functions that Andreas rated as 'very important' below and then look at the *Contents* page of *Business Result Intermediate Student's Book*. Based on this information and what you know about Andreas from the DVD, which parts of the book do you think will be especially important to use with Andreas?

- *discuss projects you are working on*
- *talk about free time and hobbies*
- *explain how something works*
- *present and discuss plans*
- *discuss and make decisions*
- *describe processes and make appointments*

_____

_____

_____

7 ▶ Watch this section. Does the teacher agree with your views in **6**?

_____

_____

Materials used in the lesson

- *Business Result Intermediate Student's Book*, Unit 5, pages 30–31, exercises 2 and 6
- *Oxford Advanced Learner's Dictionary*

Part 1 | What kind of vocabulary do we teach in business English?

1 Here are ten words you might need to teach. Think about when you would teach them and categorize them in the table below.

expectations	*hedge funds*	*serve*	*care*	*derivatives*
customer	*supplier*	*customer care*	*requirements*	*corporation*

I'd definitely teach this word in a general English lesson as well as in a business English lesson.	I probably wouldn't teach this word in a general English lesson, but only in a business English lesson.	I'd only teach this word in a class where the students had very specialized vocabulary needs.

2 ▶ Watch this section and answer questions 1–4.

1 John (the co-author) talks about the vocabulary in *Business Result*. Does he think it is specialized or general? Why does he think it will be relevant to many students? How do you know or decide if a word will be relevant to a student?

_____

_____

2 What kind of vocabulary does Bill (the teacher) think his students normally need to learn in his lessons? What are his reasons? Is this true for your students?

_____

_____

3 How does the teacher lead into the topic of the lesson? Is this a method you would use? Can you think of other ways to lead into the lesson?

_____

_____

4 Why is Vanda (one of the students) taking an English course? Do you think she will need any specialized vocabulary for her new job?

_____

_____

Part 2 | How do we teach new vocabulary?

3 Read this list of activities commonly used when teaching vocabulary.
Which do you tend to use with students? Are there any which you avoid?

_____

_____

a   reading new words in a text
b   matching words to pictures
c   completing a text with missing words
d   identifying the stressed syllables
e   matching words to collocations
f   looking words up in a dictionary
g   building words into their different forms (verb, adjective, noun)
h   writing sentences with new words
i   asking and answering questions using new words
j   giving mini-presentations which require use of new words
k   trying different ways of recording new words in a vocabulary notebook

4 ▶ Watch this section and answer questions 1–5.

1   Which activity from **3** does Bill ask the students to do first?

_____

2   How does John believe you make vocabulary meaningful for students' work?

_____

3   What other activity from **3** does Bill use?

_____

4   Which activities from **3** does Vanda mention?

_____

5   Which techniques does Bill recommend?

_____

5 Here are two statements from this section of the DVD. Are they true for you?
Are they only true sometimes? Edit or rewrite the statements if necessary.

❝ You present the vocabulary in a meaningful
context ... then you need to practise the vocabulary
in a controlled way and then in a free way ... **❞**

❝ Quite often I see students come with a
bilingual dictionary ... [but] ... they need a
good English-English dictionary. **❞**

6 Here are the bullet points from the final screen. Can you add two more bullets to
the list of tips and advice?
- contextualize the new vocabulary
- make it relevant to the students' work
- teach the meaning, form, and pronunciation
- let the students personalize the vocabulary

- _____

- _____

Material used in the lesson

- *Business Result Intermediate Student's Book*, Unit 5, page 32, exercises 4, 5, and 6
- *Business Result Intermediate Audio CD*

Part 1 | Is there a special kind of English for telephoning?

1 List three types of telephone calls you have made in the last few days (e.g. call to a friend to arrange to meet).

_____

2 Now answer the following questions for each call.

- How formal or informal was each one?

_____

- Did you use language you would only use in a phone call (e.g. *Can I speak to …*)?

_____

- Were there any difficulties (e.g. the other person understanding what you wanted)?

_____

- If you made the calls in another language, what other difficulties would you have?

_____

Sergio Yes, of course. Actually, we're coming to Switzerland next month.

Elena Really?

Sergio Yes, we already have another client in Zurich. Is that near you?

Elena Not too far. I'm in Bern. It's only a couple of hours away.

Sergio Fine. Can we arrange a meeting then?

Elena Sure.

Sergio Let's see. Well, my trip begins on the 30th of January. That's a Monday. How about Tuesday the 31st?

Elena I'd prefer the Wednesday.

Sergio The 1st of February? Yes, that suits me.

3 Read the telephone conversation on the left from *Unit 5* and answer questions 1–2.

1 Is there any language in the dialogue that is specific to the telephone or could the whole conversation also take place in a face-to-face situation?

_____

2 What difficulties might students encounter when having a similar conversation on the telephone as opposed to face-to-face?

_____

4 Imagine you are going to play this dialogue in class. Write three comprehension questions for students to answer.

1 _____?

2 _____?

3 _____?

5 ▶ Watch this section and answer questions 1–2.

1 Does the co-author believe there is a special kind of English for telephoning?

_____

2 Did the teacher ask her students to answer any of your comprehension questions in **4**?

_____

Part 2 | Why do students need English for the telephone?

6 Have you ever taught a student who needed English for telephoning? What did the student communicate about on the phone? Who did the student communicate with?

_____

7 ▶ Watch this section and answer questions 1–3.

1 Why does the student (Gianluca) need to use English on the telephone?

_____

2 What are five useful expressions you could teach him?

_____

3 What kind of role-play situation would he benefit from practising in class?

_____

Part 3 | What are the difficulties for students?

8 ▶ Watch this section and tick which person mentions the difficulties.

	author	student	teacher
no visual cues	✓		
understanding words / key content			
pronunciation / accents			
lack of confidence			
using key expressions			

9 What specific difficulties do your students have with telephoning? How have you tried to help them?

_____

10 Read the tips below for telephone role-plays. Do you agree with the tips? Would you add any more?

Tips for effective telephone role-plays

1 Give them a model of the target conversation (through listening).
2 Provide key expressions beforehand.
3 Give a structure to follow where possible.
4 Provide a realistic and relevant scenario.
5 Let students add their own ideas to the scenario.
6 If you can't use real phones in class, make sure students don't look at each other.
7 Monitor for any problems while students role-play.
8 Spend time on feedback at the end.
9 After feedback, let students repeat and improve the role-play.

11 ▶ Watch this section again. Tick the tips that the teacher follows in her lesson.

Needs analysis

1 Possible ideas are as follows:
- the student's training manager: find out what the company's aims are for this student in the future
- the website for the student's company: get background information on what the company does, its recent history, mission statement, where in the world it does business, the type of specialist vocabulary used in the business
- the student's line manager: what he or she would like the student to do in English, any areas of difficulty or any future changes in role that may require specific English
- the results from the placement test: the level and particular areas of difficulty
- the student's job description: find out day-to-day roles
- a report from the student's previous English course tutor: useful information on level and perhaps how the student likes to learn
- copies of correspondence received in the student's department: what written communication the student deals with and perhaps samples of the student's own writing
- the names of other companies that the student does business with: this may indicate what nationalities the student communicates in English with and the type of business content.

2 1 A first day analysis using the *Needs analysis form*, which can be filled in by the student or used to interview the student.

2 Name, name of the company and the nature of its business, job title, his day-to-day responsibilities, his previous learning, how he likes to learn English.

3 Andreas prefers one-to-one lessons because they are more effective and the teacher can correct his specific errors.

3 1 A needs analysis needs to find out the student's level (using a placement test) and answer the following questions.
- What do you communicate about?
- Who do you communicate with?
- How do you communicate?

2 Andreas communicates with clients and colleagues in Germany. He also communicates with partners in English. He communicates in English with both native (British and American) and non-native speakers (Polish, Dutch, Italian). He finds it easier to understand British speakers. He thinks fluency is more important and it's OK to make a few mistakes. He'd like to be corrected after an exercise in class. Speaking is more important than writing, although he does need to write emails. He needs specialist English relating to IT and then general English for making small talk, etc.

4 Possible comments are as follows.

Strengths	Weaknesses
Andreas seems quite confident and reasonably fluent for the level.	He has quite a strong accent with some pronunciation problems typical to German speakers, including his initial mispronunciation of his company (*Finanz IT*).
He talks about his work quite easily and is able to self correct	He uses the past tense instead of the present tense (… *our company developed and produced IT systems* …).
His errors don't interfere with understanding.	He makes errors with superlatives (*effectiveist, at the best*).
	He makes other minor errors (*to listen them, some basis English, the teacher see*).

5 Answers will vary.

6 & 7 The teacher suggests that Andreas will need to focus on business communication skills, such as meetings, telephoning, and socializing. These skills are covered in the middle sections of each unit. He also needs to work on emails, so she would set him tasks from the *Interactive Workbook* to do outside of class. She'll use topics from the *Student's Book* on Services & systems (*Unit 4*), Processes (*Unit 14*), Innovation (*Unit 12*), and Leisure time (*Unit 3*).

Vocabulary

1 How you answered will depend on your teaching context, but words such as *hedge funds* and *derivatives* are quite specialized and would only normally be of interest to business people working in financial sectors. Words like *supplier, corporation,* and *customer care* are typically presented in business English course books, whereas words such as *serve,* or *care* could easily appear in a general English lesson. As always, what words you choose to teach will be affected by the needs of the students.

2 1 The author suggests that the vocabulary in *Business Result* is high frequency in many parts of the business world, so it can be used with groups of students from different business backgrounds. One way to find out if a word is relevant for a student is to ask them if they would use it in their job, or ask them to make a sentence using the word related to their work. You can also look at documentation they use at work and see if it is included.

2 Bill tends to teach more general vocabulary because he finds that his students already know the words for their specialist areas of business. Many teachers also say the same thing, although this doesn't mean that we won't have to teach specialist vocabulary at some stage.

3 The teacher tells the students that the topic of the lesson is 'customer care' and asks them to talk about good or bad experiences of customer service. In this way he finds out what students already know about the topic and when they talk he can hear what sort of vocabulary they are already using. For example, Vanda uses the word *expectations* in her description of poor customer care, which is a word the teacher plans to teach in this lesson.

4 Vanda is preparing for a new job in an international publishing house. She may need some industry-specific vocabulary related to this.

3 Answers will vary.

4 1 c

2 By asking them to personalize it

3 d

4 a, f, h

5 Bill describes how he asks students to use dictionaries and write sentences which are relevant to them. We also see Bill ask students to put words in a text and answer questions with the words.

5 In the first statement, the co-author proposes a classic Presentation-Practice-Production structure for teaching new words. However, there can be drawbacks with this. For example, students may already know the words you present. In one-to-one teaching words are often taught as the lesson proceeds or as they come up. There has been a great deal of debate on this topic and many alternative ways of teaching vocabulary have been suggested.

The second statement raises the issue of dictionary use and how and when students should use either a bilingual dictionary or an English-English dictionary. Perhaps the best solution is to allow both in the classroom.

6 Other possible tips might include the following.
• teach collocations with the word
• train students to record the new words in different ways
• recycle, recycle, recycle

Telephoning

1 & 2 Calls might include giving bank details, questioning a payment, booking tickets, etc. Even in our own language, we can have difficulties, such as interference on the line with a mobile phone, having to explain something quite complex, or even understanding the accent of someone from another part of the country. In another language there are also the problems of pronunciation, unexpected responses, unknown vocabulary and expressions, different protocols on the phone, or needing clarification.

3 1 There is no language which might not also occur in a face-to-face situation.

2 The lack of body language makes the conversation more difficult. For example, without a nod of understanding or even people looking at a diary together, students can be less confident they understand what is being agreed.

4 Answers will vary.

5 1 The author believes that there is a special kind of English for telephoning, but that this is quite minimal.

2 Answers will vary.

6 Answers will vary.

7 1 Gianluca needs to use English on the telephone when speaking to partners in Germany. He has to talk about price, materials, and delivery.

2 Some expressions he might need are as follows.
How much …?
Can you give me your prices for …?
I can offer you …
I'll call our warehouse and call you back.

3 He would benefit from role-plays involving a customer or partner enquiring about a delivery.

8

	author	student	teacher
no visual cues	✓		
understanding words / key content	✓	✓	✓
pronunciation / accents	✓	✓	
lack of confidence			✓
using key expressions			✓

9 & 10 Answers will vary.

11 1 ✓

2 ✓

3 ✓

4 This isn't clear from the DVD, however 'arranging to meet' is likely to be a realistic and relevant scenario.

5 This isn't clear from the DVD.

6 ✓

7 We don't see this on the DVD, however the teacher gives feedback on expressions afterwards so she must have monitored.

8 ✓

9 We don't see this on the DVD, but at the end the teacher mentions that she will need to do much more role-play in order to build confidence.